Lively Bible Lessons for Preschoolers

(revised and updated)

Group
Loveland, Colorado

Group's R.E.A.L. Guarantee® to you:

This Group resource incorporates our R.E.A.L. approach to ministry—one that encourages long-term retention and life transformation. It's ministry that's:

Relational
Because learner-to-learner interaction enhances learning and builds Christian friendships.

Experiential
Because what learners experience through discussion and action sticks with them up to 9 times longer than what they simply hear or read.

Applicable
Because the aim of Christian education is to equip learners to be both hearers and doers of God's Word.

Learner-based
Because learners understand and retain more when the learning process takes into consideration how they learn best.

Lively Bible Lessons for Preschoolers (revised and updated)

Copyright © 1991 and 2004 by Group Publishing, Inc.

2004 edition

Visit our Web site: **www.grouppublishing.com**

Credits

Editors: Cindy S. Hansen and Mikal Keefer
Contributors: Karen M. Ball, Patti Chromey, Nanette Goings, Jerayne Gray-Reneberg, Ray and Cindy Peppers, Jolene L. Roehlkepartain, Jane P. Wilke, Paul Woods, and Christine Yount
Cover Designer: Bambi Morehead
Print Production Artist: Joyce Douglas
Illustrator: Helen H. Harrison
Production Manager: Peggy Naylor

Library of Congress Cataloging-in-Publication Data
Lively Bible Lessons for Preschoolers/edited by Cindy S. Hansen.
     p. cm.
1. Bible—Study. 2. Children—Religious life. 3. Children—Conduct of life. I. Hansen, Cindy S. II. Group Books (Firm)
BS600.2.L533   1991
268'.432—cd2   91-21658
ISBN 0-7644-2543-9
10 9 8 7 6 5 4 3 2 1   06 05 04
Printed in the United States of America.

Contents

PART 3: A LIVELY LOOK AT MY FAITH

PART 4: A LIVELY LOOK AT CELEBRATIONS

Introduction

Welcome to a resource filled with lively, active Bible lessons for your preschool children ages three to five. Here are fun sessions that'll hold your kids' attention and teach self-esteem-building, friendship-boosting, faith-developing topics.

Lively Bible Lessons for Preschoolers offers Sunday school teachers, vacation Bible school teachers, and any leader of young children twenty simple-to-follow lessons that combine lively learning, colorful art projects, and scrumptious snacks.

This book is divided into four sections:

■ **Part 1: A Lively Look at Myself**—Preschoolers are growing and facing new experiences daily. This section covers topics that help young children with fear, responsibility, envy, and self-esteem.

■ **Part 2: A Lively Look at My Relationships**—This section helps preschoolers look past themselves to others. Topics include kindness, helping those who are hurting, sharing, friendship, feelings, and caring for God's world.

■ **Part 3: A Lively Look at My Faith**—Preschool children are interested in God, the church, and their developing faith. Faith-building topics include heaven, prayer, God's love, forgiveness, and more about God and his Son, Jesus.

■ **Part 4: A Lively Look at Celebrations**—People of all ages love to celebrate special occasions. This section offers Bible lessons and celebrations for birthdays, Easter, Thanksgiving, and Christmas.

THE LIVELY BIBLE LESSONS

Each *Lively Bible Lesson* contains eight to ten fast-paced activities. No activity lasts longer than six minutes. Lessons include the following elements:

■ **Introduction**—One to two paragraphs that introduce the lesson's topic.

■ **A Powerful Purpose**—A short statement of the lesson's objective. The purpose tells you what your children will learn.

■ **A Look at the Lesson**—An outline including activity titles and estimated completion time. These times may vary depending on your group's size.

■ **A Sprinkling of Supplies**—A list of all items you'll need for the lesson. You'll probably want to keep a few general supplies in your room: crayons, paper, paints, newspapers, old shirts or smocks for paint aprons, pencils, and tape.

■ **The Lively Lesson**—Quick, active, reflective, Scripture-based activities. Lessons start with an opening experience to set the mood for the lesson. Kids experience the topics through active learning, using their senses of hearing, seeing, smelling, tasting, and feeling.

Lessons include participation Bible stories, action-packed memory verses, action songs to familiar tunes, art projects, and snacks.

■ **Handouts**—All necessary handouts are included. They're easy to use, and you have permission to photocopy them for local church use.

Enjoy *Lively Bible Lessons for Preschoolers*. Use and adapt the Bible lessons for any gathering of preschool children. Watch kids develop self-esteem, meet new friends, and grow in their faith. Have fun teaching topics in an active, lively, and meaningful way!

■ **Allergy Alert**—You'll see this symbol each time children are served food. Be aware that some children have food allergies that can be dangerous. Know your children, and consult with parents about allergies their children may have. Also be sure to read food labels carefully as hidden ingredients can cause allergy-related problems.

Part 1:
A Lively Look at Myself

What Can I Do?

A Powerful Purpose

Preschool children will understand why it's important to do our part for God.

A Look at the Lesson

E ven small children like to feel as if they have jobs all their own, or as if they're in charge. Take advantage of children's desire to be in charge, and introduce them—in an enjoyable way—to doing good things. Help them see how they can honor God by doing what pleases God.

A SPRINKLING OF SUPPLIES

- ❏ Bible
- ❏ bedsheet
- ❏ ribbon
- ❏ yarn
- ❏ crayons
- ❏ glue sticks
- ❏ hole punch
- ❏ photocopies of the handout (p. 11)
- ❏ plastic sandwich bags
- ❏ raisins
- ❏ chocolate chips
- ❏ pretzels
- ❏ large bowl
- ❏ napkins
- ❏ juice
- ❏ cups
- ❏ scissors

You'll also need enough metal spoons and pan lids for your whole class.

THE LIVELY LESSON

1. Our Band

(You'll need the metal spoons and pan lids.) Form children into two groups. Give each child in the first group two spoons. Give each child in the second group two pan lids.

Thank children for coming and for being part of your band. Tell them you're glad they're here!

Once everyone has an "instrument," organize your band. All spoons sit together; all lids sit together. Point to the spoons and let them play their best! Motion for them to stop, then point to the lids and have them play their best. Motion for them to stop.

Tell band members you also want them to sing. Have them put their instruments down on the floor, then practice singing "Hallelu, Hallelu." Assign one half the "Hallelu" part and the other half the "Praise ye the Lord" part. Practice singing the song "Hallelu, Hallelu." If you don't know this song, teach kids another praise chorus you know.

After kids know the song, add instruments and make a joyful noise to the Lord.

2. Do Your Part

Gather the instruments, then have kids sit in a circle. SAY: **Everyone who sang the "Hallelu" part in the song, raise your hand.** (Pause.) **Now everyone who sang the "Praise ye the Lord" part, raise your hand.** (Pause.) **What would have happened if we reached the "Praise ye the Lord" part and no one sang? Would the song be as much fun? Let's try it and see.**

Sing the song one time through without the "Praise ye the Lord" part.

SAY: **That wasn't as much fun as before, was it? It was kind of confusing, too. We weren't sure when we were supposed to sing. We needed everyone to do his or her part. Doing what we say we'll do is important. It's like keeping a promise.**

ASK: **What happens when you don't keep a promise?**

Listen to answers such as "People get angry" and "We hurt people."

3. Partner Pals

Form pairs by having everyone hold the hand of someone sitting close by. Have one child in each pair close his or her eyes. Have the other child lead his or her partner around the room, making sure the child doesn't run into anything or any other person. Stress that kids' jobs are to take care of their partners.

After about a minute, have partners switch. Allow about another minute for them to walk around the room together.

4. Being Faithful

(You'll need a Bible.)

SAY: **Good job taking care of your partners! You did your jobs well.**

Gather in a circle again. Ask:

• **What could have happened if you hadn't led your partner carefully?**

• **Why is it important to do what you're supposed to?**

SAY: **You did great! Your partners didn't run into anything; they were safe. You cared for your partners. You did your part. That's what God wants us to do.**

Read Proverbs 21:3a: **"Do what is right and just." Let's say this Bible verse together.**

Lead children in saying the verse together a couple times, then ASK:

• **How do you know the right thing to do?**

• **Who helps you know what's right to do?**

SAY: **God is pleased when we do what's right.**

5. Team Tug

(You'll need an old bedsheet.)

If the weather is nice, play this game outside on a grassy area. If not, play on soft carpet. Inside, ask kids to remove their shoes and play in their socks.

Form two teams. Twist the sheet so it's in the shape of a rope and play Tug of War. After each round, move children to different teams so that all the children have a chance to be on the winning team. Do at least two or three rounds, then have children sit down.

ASK: **Why was it hard to pull on the sheet?**

SAY: **Just like it was hard to pull against another team, it's also hard to do what's right sometimes. Suppose your mom tells you to clean your room but your friends ask you to play. Or what if you're supposed to help set the table for dinner but you want to watch TV? It's not always easy to do what we're supposed to do.**

ASK: **How can we help each other do our part?**

Listen to answers such as "Pray for each other," "Help each other," "Share," "Don't ask someone to play if you know he's supposed to be helping his mom." Tell kids to go around the circle, and one at a time call each child by name to say, "Help each other."

6. Our Part

(You'll need crayons, ribbon, different colors of yarn, glue sticks, and photocopies of the "Our Part" handout. Cut out the face on the handout, and use a hole punch to punch a hole in top.)

Give one handout and crayons to each child. Read the words on it: **"Do what is right and just."** Let children draw their own faces in the circles and then glue yarn on for hair. Help kids thread ribbons through the holes so that they can hang the pictures up at home to remind themselves that it's important to do what's right.

7. Responsible Snacks

(You'll need a separate plastic sandwich bag filled with one of these items for each child: chocolate chips, raisins, pretzels. You'll also need a large bowl, napkins, juice, and cups.)

Give each person a plastic bag filled with an item to make trail mix. SAY: **Each one of us has an ingredient for our snack. It's your part to put your ingredient in this big bowl.**

Ask one person to put his or her ingredient in the bowl. SAY: **If no one did his or her part to add to the snack, would it be as good? We each need to do our job.**

Mix the goodies and serve the trail mix on napkins. Give everyone juice to drink. Close the lesson by praying: **God, help us to do our part. Help us do what's right. Remind us to help our friends do their part too. We love you. Amen.**

by Karen M. Ball

Our Part

"Do what is right and just."
(Proverbs 21:3a)

Green With Envy

A Powerful Purpose

Preschool children will learn to be happy with the things they have, not envious of other people's things.

A Look at the Lesson

1. Look at My Snack . . . . (up to 10 minutes)
2. Envious Faces . . . . (up to 4 minutes)
3. Flannel Board Photos . . . . (up to 5 minutes)
4. Good for You . . . . (up to 6 minutes)
5. My Blessings . . . . (up to 6 minutes)
6. Love Is Not Envious . . . . (up to 5 minutes)
7. A Taste of Envy . . . . (up to 6 minutes)

E nvy is a common feeling for all people, all ages. Many adults closely watch for the newest and neatest gadgets and technology, as well as the new items their neighbors buy. Little children play with their toys but want their friends' toys.

Use this lesson to help young children deal with envy. Teach preschoolers to give thanks for what they have.

A SPRINKLING OF SUPPLIES

- ☐ Bible
- ☐ brownies
- ☐ small crackers
- ☐ paper
- ☐ marker
- ☐ flannel board
- ☐ pictures of Joseph and his special coat
- ☐ crayons
- ☐ red gelatin
- ☐ table knives
- ☐ napkins
- ☐ paper plates

THE LIVELY LESSON

1. Look at My Snack

(You'll need brownies and small crackers. Use a marker to draw a huge smile on a piece of paper. Draw a huge frown on another piece of paper.)

When kids arrive, gather them in a circle and distribute snacks. Half of the class receives brownies, while the other half receives crackers. SAY: **A brownie for you, a cracker for you** as you hand them out.

You'll likely hear protests from the cracker receivers, but just bear with them.

Hold up the smile and ASK: **How many of you felt like this when I gave you a snack? Why?** Let kids respond with "I love brownies" or "They taste great."

Hold up the frown and ASK: **How many of you felt like this? Why?** Let them respond with "I like brownies better than crackers" or "The brownie was bigger. I was hungry."

Give crackers to the children who already received brownies and brownies to the children who already received crackers. SAY: **Remember, all good things come from God.**

Tell children that there's a word to describe our feelings when we want something someone else has. It's called *envy*. We feel envy when we want others' things instead of thinking of our own good gifts.

2. Envious Faces

Let everyone practice smiling and frowning. Then SAY: **I'm going to read some situations. If one makes you happy, show me a big smile. If one makes you feel sad, angry, or full of envy, show me a big frown.**

Read these situations:

• **Your sister just got a brand-new tricycle, and you didn't get anything.**

• **A friend is eating a juicy apple; he gives you one too.**

• **Your baby brother is surrounded by aunts and uncles who are oohing and aahing. Nobody notices you.**

• **A next-door neighbor is playing with a brand-new red truck in his brand-new sandbox. He doesn't ask you to play.**

• **You're holding your favorite book. You offer to show it to your friend.**

• **Your teacher tells you that you're going**

to hear a good Bible story.

3. Flannel Board Photos

(You'll need a flannel board and pictures from the story about Joseph and his special coat. Use flannel board pictures from Sunday school resources or pictures from a children's Bible or storybook. Make your own flannel board by covering a sturdy piece of cardboard—any size you want—with light-colored flannel. Glue a small piece of flannel to the back of each picture you'll use.)

Before you start the story, give kids a stretch break with the following chant. Have kids follow you in doing the actions.

Smile (*stand and smile*),
Frown (*bend your knees and frown*),
Smile (*stand and smile*),
Frown (*bend your knees and frown*),
Now it's time to sit back down. (*Sit down by the flannel board.*)

Tell the story of Joseph, his special coat, and his envious brothers by reading Genesis 37:3-4, 14, 18-28. Let the children use the flannel board pictures to help you tell the story. If time permits, tell the story again and let different children move the pictures on the board.

4. Good for You

SAY: **Those brothers felt a lot of envy because Joseph's dad liked him best. Joseph got a bright-colored coat, and his brothers didn't. Sometimes we feel envy just like Joseph's brothers when we don't get what we want.**

Give kids a chance to say things that make them envious. For example, when a friend gets a new toy and they don't. Then tell them that they're going to change envy into a good feeling. Tell kids you'll stand up and say some sort of good news, then sit down. After each bit of good news, kids are to stand up and say, "I'm glad for you," then sit back down. SAY:

• **Look! My dad just gave me roller skates.**

• **My grandma is coming to take me to the zoo!**

• **My mom lets me stay up late on Friday nights.**

Add some of the situations kids previously said made them envious. After each item you say, encourage kids to say, "I'm glad for you!"

SAY: **Sometimes it isn't easy to be glad for others when they get something we'd like, but that's what God wants us to do.**

5. My Blessings

(For each child, you'll need a piece of paper and crayons.)

Distribute paper to the children. Tell them each to draw a picture of a blessing—a favorite toy, pet, or somewhere nice they've been on vacation. When they finish, let them share their pictures with the others.

After each child shares, have everyone else stand up and say, "I'm glad for you."

Emphasize that God blesses all of us with gifts. None of us should envy others.

6. Love Is Not Envious

Have kids learn this memory verse from 1 Corinthians 13:4a: "Love is patient, love is kind. It does not envy." Have kids repeat the verse with you, using the motions. Work with them until they can say it by themselves with you just leading the motions.

Love is patient (hug yourself),

Love is kind. (Draw a smile on your face with both pointer fingers.)

It does not (shake your head "no")

envy. (Make a frown on your face.)

7. A Taste of Envy

(You'll need a shallow pan of red gelatin, table knives, and napkins. Prepare the gelatin according to the "Jigglers" recipe on the package.)

Help children each cut a large crescent shape out of the gelatin and put it on a paper plate. Have them each hold their crescent shape like a frown as you SAY: **God doesn't want us to be envious. It makes God sad when we envy others.**

Then have kids each hold their crescent shape like a smile. SAY: **God wants us to be happy when others are happy. It makes God happy when we don't envy others. Let's gobble up any envy we may have.**

Encourage kids to gobble up their crescents.

Serve kids any leftovers.

Close with a prayer: **Thank you, God, for all our blessings. Take envy away and make us happy for others. Amen.**

by Ray and Cindy Peppers

frightening fears

A Powerful Purpose

Preschool children will recognize that they don't have to be afraid because God protects them.

A Look at the Lesson

A child's world can be full of frightening things. Children don't think there's a huge, hairy, sharp-toothed monster under their bed; they know it!

Use this lesson to put fears in a new light. Let young children see they can get rid of their fears and give them to God. Help children see that God is bigger than their fears.

THE LIVELY LESSON

1. Don't Be Afraid

(You'll need one blindfold.)

Welcome children and tell them you're going to play a game called Don't Be Afraid.

Blindfold one child. Have the other children walk in a circle around the blindfolded child. Tell the blindfolded child to try to walk out of the circle without running into anyone. When the child is about to run into someone, yell, "Stop, kids! Don't be afraid." Then have the

A SPRINKLING OF SUPPLIES

- [ ] Bible
- [ ] blindfold
- [ ] paper
- [ ] marker
- [ ] doll
- [ ] large box
- [ ] trash can
- [ ] crayons
- [ ] ribbon
- [ ] stickers
- [ ] photocopies of the handout (p. 18)
- [ ] small box of raisins for each child
- [ ] trash bag filled with heavy books

other children squeeze together and hug the blindfolded child. Remove the blindfold and give it to another child to continue the game.

SAY: **God tells us the same thing when we're afraid: "Stop, kids! Don't be afraid. I'm here to help you."**

2. Fears Drag You Down

(You'll need a trash bag filled with heavy books—heavy enough so kids have some difficulty dragging it, but not so heavy that it causes muscle strain.)

Tell children they're going to run a short relay race that'll show them how their fears can keep them from doing their best.

Form two teams. Help teams line up at one end of the room. Give one team the heavy bag of books. Tell that team that— one person at a time—team members have to drag the bag across the room and back. The other team's members can run freely. One at a time, team members each run across the room and back and then tag the next person on their team, who repeats the process. Continue until everyone has run. First team done wins.

After the first race, give the bag of books to the other team and race again.

Afterward ASK: **Which was harder—running by yourself or dragging the bag? How did you feel dragging the bag?**

SAY: **Fear is like that heavy, old bag. It keeps us from doing our best, even from doing things we really want to do. Fear can keep us from doing things God wants us to do.**

3. Fear List

(You'll need a piece of paper for each child and a marker.)

Ask kids to name their fears. Some possibilities are the dark, monsters, getting lost, parents getting a divorce, a war.

Write one fear on each piece of paper. After you write one fear for each child, wad it and toss it to a child. SAY: **[Name], grab that fear!** After each child has caught a fear, SAY: **Now we'll try to get rid of our fears.**

4. Fear Bombardment

(You'll need a doll, a large box, and the wads of paper fears.)

Place a doll in the center of the room. Gather kids in a circle around it. SAY: **Pretend that doll is a person who's afraid of all these fears. She's hit with them daily.**

Let kids throw their paper fears at the doll.

Next, place a large box over the doll. Ask kids to pick up a paper fear and get back to the circle. Tell them to throw the fears again and try to hit the doll.

SAY: **Our fears are like these paper wads raining down on the doll. They come at us fast and hit us. But when the doll was covered by the box, the fears couldn't hit her. She was protected. God helps us like that box helped her. He covers us with his love and protection.**

5. Fear Protection

(You'll need a Bible.)

ASK: **Who protects us from our fears?** Answers could be God, Jesus, parents, friends.

Tell the story of David and Goliath found in 1 Samuel 17.

SAY: **In the Bible, David was sometimes afraid. But he knew God would protect him. Listen to David's words.**

Read Psalm 27:1 from a children's Bible, or use this wording: **"The Lord is my light** and the one who saves me. I fear no one. The Lord protects my life. I am afraid of no one."

David knew that God was stronger than anything or anyone else. All we need to do is ask God to cover us—to protect us. Then the fears can't get to us. With God's help and protection, we don't need to be afraid.

6. Get Rid of Those Fears

(You'll need the wadded paper fears and a trash can.)

Gather the paper wads of fear, unwad them, and read them aloud. After each fear you read, have kids say, "I'm not afraid. God protects me."

Throw the fears in a trash can and SAY: **God gets rid of our fears.**

7. I'm Not Alone

Gather kids in a circle and stand in the middle. SAY: **Our family and friends also help protect us from our fears. When we're afraid, we can tell them about it. And we can ask them to pray with us. Their love can surround and protect us. It's easier to not be afraid when we remember we're not alone.**

Choose one person to come stand in the middle with you. Both of you SAY: **We're not alone.** Have that child choose another child to come stand in the middle with you and all three of you SAY: **We're not alone.** Continue until everyone is chosen and bunched together.

8. God's Protective Love

(You'll need crayons, ribbon, tape, stickers, and other decorations. Each child will need a small closed-up box of raisins and a photocopy of the "God's Box of Protective Love" handout.)

Tell kids they're going to decorate their own boxes to remind them that God covers them with his protective love. Give them each a box and a handout. Read the words to them: **Don't be afraid, [Name]. God loves you and protects you.**

Give kids the decorating supplies. Let them color and decorate their boxes any way they want. While they're decorating, give specific words of praise as you go around to each one. Tape a handout-card to each box. Write the child's name in the space provided.

9. Thanks for God's Love

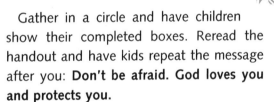

Gather in a circle and have children show their completed boxes. Reread the handout and have kids repeat the message after you: **Don't be afraid. God loves you and protects you.**

Pray: **Thank you, Father, for loving us and for being our protection against things that make us afraid. Help us to trust you. Help us not to be afraid. Amen.**

Let children open their boxes and eat their raisins.

by Karen M. Ball

God's Box of Protective Love

Don't be afraid,

_____.

God loves you and protects you.

God's Box of Protective Love

Don't be afraid,

_____.

God loves you and protects you.

What Makes Me Special?

A Powerful Purpose

Preschool children will realize that each of us is special to God and to each other.

A Look at the Lesson

1. Run Around . . . . (up to 6 minutes)
2. Let's Make a Snowflake . . . . (up to 6 minutes)
3. Beach Ball Roll . . . . (up to 5 minutes)
4. Very Good . . . . (up to 5 minutes)
5. Happy-Face Stickers . . . . (up to 4 minutes)
6. Hugging Game . . . . (up to 4 minutes)
7. God Says I'm Special . . . . (up to 6 minutes)
8. Happy-Face Snack . . . . (up to 5 minutes)

A SPRINKLING OF SUPPLIES

- ❏ CD of lively music
- ❏ CD player
- ❏ white paper
- ❏ safety scissors
- ❏ beach ball
- ❏ Bible
- ❏ happy-face stickers
- ❏ crayons
- ❏ photocopies of the handout (p. 22)
- ❏ milk
- ❏ cups
- ❏ napkins
- ❏ cookies or cupcakes with frosting happy faces

Children are unique and wonderful. Jesus tells his disciples to "let the little children come to me." In fact, they're so special that Jesus said "the kingdom of heaven belongs to such as these" (Matthew 19:14).

Use this lesson to celebrate how God has made each of us special and unique. Reassure children that God's love for them is unlimited.

THE LIVELY LESSON

1. Run Around

(You'll need a soundtrack of lively music and a CD player.)

Have children jog around the room as you play music. Have children freeze where they are and all call out their names at the same time when you stop the music. The last child to say his or her name joins you and helps you stop the music and claps for those still playing.

Start the music again, and keep going in this manner until there's only one child left jogging. Vary the game by changing the actions kids do to the music. Have them skip, hop, walk, and tiptoe.

SAY: **You all are special. You played a fun game and clapped for each other. We're going to learn more about what makes us special and wonderful creations.**

2. Let's Make a Snowflake

(For each child, fold one square piece of white paper in half from top to bottom, in half again from side to side, in half diagonally to form a triangle, and in half diagonally again. Each child will need a safety scissors.)

Ask children to sit in a circle. SAY: **Each of us is special. There's no one else like us anywhere in the world. Even people who look alike, such as identical twins, are different inside. We're like snowflakes. Did you know that no two snowflakes look exactly alike? Let's make some snowflakes and check that out.**

Snowflakes

Give children folded paper and safety scissors. Show them how to make snowflakes by cutting small pieces away from the outside edges. You may need to help children make their cuts. Then open to reveal the snowflake. Compare kids' snowflakes to see if any are alike. Put each child's name on his or her snowflake.

3. Beach Ball Roll

(You'll need a beach ball.)

SAY: **Just like the snowflakes, we're all different. We all have things that make us special.**

ASK: **What are some things that make us special?**

Talk about things we can *do* such as singing, playing, smiling, laughing, praying, or helping; things that we *are* such as children, daughters, sons, cheerful, smart, or helpful; even physical characteristics such as eye color, hair color, freckles, strong, or graceful.

Go around the circle and let each person say one thing that makes him or her special.

SAY: **Let's play a game. I'll roll a ball to someone. The person who catches the ball must say one thing that makes him or her special. That person rolls the ball to someone else who does the same. We'll continue until everyone has a turn.**

Be ready to help kids out if they can't think of anything.

4. Very Good

(You'll need a Bible.)

Say: **God made us the way we are. He made everything on the earth. What are some of God's creations?**

Let kids respond with things such as heaven, earth, animals, sky, water, flowers, trees, and fish.

Tell the story of Creation from Genesis 1.

SAY: **God made all of these things. After he made each one, he said it was good. And after God made people, he looked at his creation and said it was very good. God thinks we all are very special because he made us to be like him.**

Read Genesis 1:31 from a children's Bible,

or read this wording: **"God looked at everything he had made, and it was very good."**

Ask kids to go around the room, shake each other's hands, and say, "God thinks you're very good."

5. Happy-Face Stickers

(You'll need a happy-face sticker for each person.)

SAY: **We need to remind each other that we're special.**

ASK: **What are some ways we can do that?**

Help kids think of ways such as hugging, kissing, saying thank you, giving a gift, doing something nice for a person.

Divide into pairs by saying: **I'll count to three. In those three seconds, you have to grab the hand of someone who's standing close by you. But you can only hold one other hand. Ready? One, two, three. Got a partner?**

Give each child a happy-face sticker. Have each child put the sticker on his or her partner's hand and say, "Smile, you're special."

6. Hugging Game

(You'll need a CD of lively music and a CD player.)

Ask children to stand in a circle, facing inward. Play the lively music. Have one child walk around the outside of the circle, gently patting each child on the back as he or she passes, until the music stops. When the music stops, have the child hug the person he or she is behind and say, "You're

special." Then have those two children switch places and continue the game.

Let each person have a chance to walk around the circle. Play until each child has been hugged.

7. God Says I'm Special

(You'll need crayons and the "God Says I'm Special" handout.)

Give each person a handout and crayons. SAY: **This handout says "God Says I'm Special" across the top. There's space for you to draw your picture. The words say, "Just like snowflakes, God made me and I'm special." Genesis 1:31 is written on the bottom. Remember, God created people and said they were very good—very special.**

Let kids draw their pictures. If you want, you could take kids' pictures with an instant-print or digital camera and place them on the handouts instead of having kids draw.

8. Happy-Face Snack

(For each child, you'll need a cookie or cupcake with a frosting happy face on it. You'll also need milk, cups, and napkins.)

Serve the happy-face snack. Before kids eat, pray: **God, thanks for making us special. Help us remember how much you love us and how special that makes us. Amen.**

Have children take the pictures and snowflakes home, or post them on a bulletin board titled "God's Special Creations."

by Karen M. Ball

God Says I'm Special

Just like snowflakes,
God made me and I'm special!

Share Genesis 1:31 with your preschooler!

Part 2: A Lively Look at My Relationships

Friends Forever

A Powerful Purpose

Preschool children will learn
that everybody can be a friend.

A Look at the Lesson

As preschool children progress, their social development changes. According to Mary Irene Flanagan, author of the *Preschool Handbook*, three-year-olds like being with other children but still like to play alone. Four-year-olds begin to show a growing interest in doing things with other children. And by the time children turn five, they seek affection from their peers and like to play in small groups.

As preschool children develop socially, they need to understand the importance of friendship. Use this lesson to help preschoolers learn how to be a friend.

THE LIVELY LESSON

1. Beanbag Catch

(You'll need a beanbag.)

Have children sit in a circle. Give one child a beanbag and tell the child to say his or her name before saying, "is a friend." The child then gently tosses the beanbag to another child in the circle who says his or her name

A SPRINKLING OF SUPPLIES

- ❒ Bible
- ❒ crayons
- ❒ paper
- ❒ one beanbag
- ❒ red and pink construction paper
- ❒ poster board
- ❒ pennies
- ❒ string
- ❒ Cheerios
- ❒ juice
- ❒ cups
- ❒ scissors

before saying, "is a friend," and tosses the beanbag to another child. For example, if Steven gets the beanbag first, he says, "Steven is a friend" and tosses it to Janie who says, "Janie is a friend," before tossing it to another child.

After playing the game for about three minutes, SAY: **Each one of us is a friend. And now we're going to say that the other children here are friends.**

Play the game again, only change the game by having the child say the name of the person he or she tosses the beanbag to instead of his or her own name. For example, if Steven gets the beanbag first, he says, "Janie is a friend" before tossing the beanbag to her.

After the game SAY: **Isn't it great that we're all friends? God is happy when we're all good friends.**

2. Good News About Friends

SAY: **The Bible has some good news about friends. In Proverbs 17:17 it says, "A friend loves at all the times."**

Have children pat each other lightly on the back as they say the verse with you several times. SAY: **We can show love to our friends all the time.**

3. Friendship Singalong

Have children sing together these words to the tune of "Skip to My Lou." Ask children to point to themselves when they refer to themselves in the song and point to another child when singing "you." Join hands on the last line.

I'm a friend and that is true.
I'm a friend and that is true.
I'm a friend and that is true.
I'm a friend forever.

You're a friend and that is true.
You're a friend and that is true.
You're a friend and that is true.
You're a friend forever.

I'm a friend and so are you.
I'm a friend and so are you.
I'm a friend and so are you.
Let's be friends together.

4. A Whale of a Friend

(Cut out hearts from red and pink construction paper. Cut enough hearts so each child has one. Fold all the hearts in half as shown on p. 27. You'll also need crayons.)

Give the children crayons and the hearts you cut from red and pink construction paper. Be sure the hearts are folded in half so they look like whales. Tell the children to decorate their whales by adding faces. After children finish, have them exchange whales with someone in the room.

SAY: **We can have a whale of a good time when we're with good friends. Now open your whales, what do you see?** (Children will see a heart.) **When we're friends, we love each other. And God wants us to be friends. Keep your whale-heart as a reminder of what good friends you have.**

5. Friendship Actions

Have children do the following actions while you read this short action story.

Everybody is a friend, and good friends stand proud. (Have children stand.)

The reason we can be proud is that God made us. Let's all shout, "Thank you for making us, God." (Have children say, "Thank you for making us, God!")

God wants us each to be a friend. And one way we can be a friend is by smiling at

the people around us. *(Have children smile at each other.)*

And by telling other people that they're good friends. *(Have children say, "You're a good friend" to the children around them.)*

Friends like to be together. They clap because they're happy. *(Have children clap.)*

They hug each other because they like each other. *(Have children hug each other.)*

And they jump for joy because everybody's a friend. *(Have children jump.)*

All this is because God made us. Let's thank God again for making us, and let's clap, too! *(Have children say, "Thanks for making us, God!" and clap at the same time.)*

6. Fantastic Friendship

Have children sit. Briefly tell the story of Jonathan and David from 1 Samuel 19:1-6. ASK: **How was Jonathan a good friend to David?**

SAY: **We're going to repeat the Bible verse in Proverbs about friendship. I'll start out the sentence, and if you remember how it ends, jump up and finish the sentence.**

SAY: **A friend loves at all_____.**

Continue to repeat the verse by leaving out one more word at the end of each line until the children know the verse well.

7. Thumbody's Friend

SAY: **Let's play a game to show that we're friends.**

Have children hold up their thumbs. Tell them to run around the room and press their thumbs against other children's thumbs and say, "I'm thumbody's friend, and that thumbody is you!"

Let the children continue this exercise until they've each interacted with most of the other children.

8. Happy Faces

(Securely tape pennies and string on a piece of poster board as shown in the "Penny Face" diagram. The pennies form the eyes and noses, the string forms the face outlines and smiles.)

Penny Face

Give each child a piece of paper and a crayon. Have children each take turns putting their piece of paper on your poster board items and rubbing gently with their crayons until the outlines and textures appear. Since pennies are a choking hazard for young children, be sure that children do not remove the pennies from the poster board. Put away the poster board as soon as this activity is completed. ASK:

• **What do you see?**

• **Why are these faces happy?**

SAY: **On our papers we see two happy faces. This is how friends look when they are together. They smile a lot. They laugh. They're happy. We can be happy like this when we're with our friends.**

9. Cheer, Cheer, Cheerios!

(You'll need Cheerios, cups, and juice.)

SAY: **Because we're happy that we have friends and that each one of us is a good friend, let's cheer three times! Then after we cheer three times, let's celebrate being friends by eating some Cheerios.**

Together cheer three times. Then serve a snack of Cheerios and juice.

10. Friendship Prayer

Ask the children to stand in a circle and link arms. SAY: **God wants us to love each other and be friends. Each one of you is special, and you're each a good friend. Now let's bow our heads and pray.**

PRAY: **God, help us to love each other and be good friends. Amen.**

by Jolene L. Roehlkepartain

Being Kind

A Powerful Purpose

Preschool children will understand the importance of kindness and practice it.

A Look at the Lesson

A SPRINKLING OF SUPPLIES

- ❏ Bible
- ❏ crayons
- ❏ photocopies of the handouts (pp. 31-32)
- ❏ scissors
- ❏ tape
- ❏ bananas
- ❏ juice
- ❏ cups
- ❏ napkins
- ❏ trash can
- ❏ animal such as a dog, cat, or rabbit

You'll also need a clothes hanger for each child.

Kindness is a quality many children don't have naturally. Selfishness is human nature; kindness is a fruit of the Spirit. "But the fruit of the Spirit is love, joy, peace, patience, kindness, goodness, faithfulness, gentleness and self-control" (Galatians 5:22-23a).

When preschoolers see kindness modeled by families, friends, and teachers, they can imitate the examples.

Use this lesson to model kindness to young children. Help them learn and use that important quality in their lives.

THE LIVELY LESSON

1. A Unique Guest

(Bring a small animal—a dog, cat, or rabbit—for children to pet. Choose a calm animal that won't get scared around the children, possibly hurting them. Also be aware of animal allergies some children may have.)

As children arrive, gather in a circle. Show them the animal, and let them take turns petting it. Show children how to pet the animal—softly, gently stroking it.

Explain to children that softly petting the animal is a way to show kindness to it.

Let everyone have a chance to show kindness to one of God's creations.

Then have someone take the animal back to its home.

2. Be Kind to Animals

Praise the children for being kind to the animal. ASK:

- **Who made animals?**
- **Why is it important that we're nice to them?**
- **Does anyone have pets at home?**
- **How can we be kind to animals?**

Allow time for kids to talk about being kind to animals by feeding them regularly, giving them plenty to drink, brushing them, and playing with them. SAY: **God made the animals. He wants us to be kind to them.**

3. Be Kind to Others

(For each child, you'll need crayons and photocopies of the "Kind Friends" handouts. Cut out the four pictures on the handouts. You'll also need a Bible.)

SAY: **God made the animals, and God also made you. God is happy when we're kind to animals. God is also happy when we're kind to each other. God wants us to be kind to others just like we were kind to the animal.**

Distribute crayons and the first picture from the "Kind Friends" handout. Briefly explain how Matthew 9:1-2, 6-8 tells us about people who were kind to their friend who couldn't walk. The friends took the paralyzed man to Jesus so Jesus could help him walk. Allow kids to color the picture.

Distribute the second picture, and tell how Jesus responded to these friends' faith.

He helped the paralyzed man walk.

Give kids the third picture, and explain to children that everyone was excited because Jesus healed the man.

After children have colored the third picture, distribute the final picture and read it to the kids: **Thank you, Jesus, for the kindness of friends.**

Let children color this final picture.

4. Mobile Stories

(You'll need tape. For each child, you'll need a clothes hanger.)

Help each child tape his or her four pictures to a clothes hanger.

After kids' mobiles are finished, help kids review the story. Point to the pictures, and let kids tell you the story by describing the pictures. ASK:

- **Who made us?**
- **Why do you think we should be kind to each other?**
- **How can we be kind to each other?**

Hang the mobile stories around the room so kids can see kindness throughout the rest of this lesson.

5. Practice Time

Lead kids in making a one-two rhythm by patting their knees, then clapping their hands. Chant these words together:

Practice time.
Practice time.
Time to practice
Being kind.

Form pairs by having kids face people who are sitting close to them. SAY: **We're going to practice being nice to each other. Shake your partner's hand and say, "I like you. You're my friend."**

Allow thirty seconds for this hand-shaking time.

SAY: **Now, tell your partner one thing you really like about him or her—for example, "I really like your smile. It makes me feel good." Or "I really like your laugh. It makes me happy."**

You may need to help children who have trouble thinking of something. Afterward, praise the children for being kind to each other.

6. Snack Exchange

(For each child, you'll need a banana, a cup of juice, and a napkin. Slice each banana at the stem to make it easier for the child to peel.)

Have children remain in pairs from the last activity. Give a banana to every child. Instruct kids to give their bananas to their partners and say, "This banana is for you. Eat and enjoy."

Praise the children for their kindness in giving each other their fruit. Allow time for them to eat.

Pour juice into a small cup for each child. Again, encourage children to give their drinks to their partners. Praise them as they successfully complete the exchange.

7. Partner Cleanup

(You'll need a trash can.)

SAY: **You've been kind to your partners by giving them a snack. Show your kindness even more by cleaning up for them.**

Let kids gather peelings, empty cups, and napkins and throw them away.

8. Kindness Prayer

Ask partners to hold hands, bow their heads, and pray silently as you PRAY: **God, thanks for friends. Help us be kind to show your love to others. Amen.**

Let kids take home their mobiles as reminders to be kind to others.

by Patti Chromey

Kind Friends

These are scenes from the story in Matthew 9:1-2, 6-8.

Friends carrying the lame man.

Jesus healing the man.

Kind Friends

Everyone's happy because he's healed.

Thank you, Jesus, for the kindness of friends. (Matthew 9:1-2, 6-8)

Learning to Share

A Powerful Purpose

Preschool children will hear a story about Elijah and learn how to share.

A Look at the Lesson

1. Create a Toy . . . . (up to 8 minutes)
2. Create a Story . . . . (up to 5 minutes)
3. The Bible Skit . . . . (up to 6 minutes)
4. Sharing a Snack With Family . . . . (up to 5 minutes)
5. Modeling Sharing . . . . (up to 4 minutes)
6. Share Our Gifts. . . . . (up to 5 minutes)
7. I Love to Share . . . . (up to 4 minutes)
8. Share Prayer . . . . (up to 3 minutes)

Preschoolers can be possessive. It's natural for children to hold onto what they have, but sharing can be learned—through patient, diligent, and consistent teaching.

Use this lesson to help kids learn to share.

THE LIVELY LESSON

1. Create a Toy

(You'll need modeling dough.)

As children arrive, greet them and tell them that you're glad they came. Give every other child a handful of modeling dough. Tell kids with dough each to share half with someone who doesn't have any.

Tell children to form the dough into the shape of a favorite toy, such as a ball or jump rope. Demonstrate with a handful of dough so kids see an example. While they're shaping their own toys, ASK:

• **Did you like sharing your modeling dough with a friend? Why or why not?**

• What did it feel like to give dough away?

• What did it feel like to receive dough?

SAY: **Sometimes it's not fun to share. I really appreciate the way you worked together. It pleases God when we share the nice things he gives us.**

2. Create a Story

(You'll need the completed modeling dough toy shapes.)

As children complete their work, ask them to sit in a large circle. SAY: **We're going to make up a story about sharing, using your dough figures. When I pause telling the story, we'll go around the circle and you'll hold up your modeling dough figure and say what it is.**

Once upon a time, God blessed some children with all kinds of toys such as... (Go around the circle and have kids name their modeling dough toy shapes.)

One day a little girl and boy moved into town. They were very poor. They didn't have many toys. They didn't have much of anything. They didn't have... (Go around and have kids name toys.)

All the children of the class met the two children and decided they wanted to share their toys with them. "Here," they said. "Play with us. Play with our..." (Go around and have kids name toys.)

The kids shared. Everyone was happy.

Have children set aside their dough toys to use later.

3. The Bible Skit

(You'll need a Bible.)

Open your Bible to 1 Kings 17:8-16. Make sure to use a translation that's easy for the children to understand. Read the story about Elijah and the widow who shared her food.

SAY: **We're going to act out this Bible story. Everybody stand up. Half of you will be Elijah, and the other half will be the widow. I'll tell you what to say and do.**

Elijah was very hungry. (Elijah group says, "I'm very hungry.")

He saw a woman. (Elijah group and widow group wave to each other.)

Elijah asked for water. (Elijah group says, "I'm thirsty. Can I have some water?")

The widow said, "OK." (Widow group says, "OK" and pretends to give water.)

Elijah asked for bread. (Elijah group says, "Can I have some bread?")

The widow said, "I barely have enough for my family" (widow group says the words),

But she did it anyway. (Widow group says, "OK. Here.")

And God kept the flour and oil coming and coming. (All say, "Thank you, God!")

The widow shared (tell widow group to wave)

With Elijah (tell Elijah group to wave),

And God blessed them both. (Everybody claps.)

4. Sharing a Snack With Family

(Prepare jam and butter sandwiches. Make two halves for each child, and place each half in a sandwich bag. You'll also need juice, cups, and napkins.)

SAY: **When the widow shared as God wanted her to, God took care of her. Often we're afraid to share our things because we're afraid we won't have them anymore. But God will always be good to us when we're kind to others and share.**

Distribute the sandwiches, two halves for each person. SAY: **Eat one now, and share** the other with your family when you go home.

Give kids juice, and let them enjoy eating the snacks.

5. Modeling Sharing

(You'll need the modeling dough toys children created earlier.)

SAY: **The Bible tells us in Luke 3:11 to share what we have with others. Let's say that together.**

Lead children in saying, "Share what you have with others."

Have children sit in a circle, and give each child one of the modeling dough toys. Each time children say the verse, have them pass the dough toys to the left. Play for about two minutes.

SAY: **God is happy when we share what we have with others.**

Put away the modeling dough.

6. Share Our Gifts

(You'll need photocopies of the "God wants you to share" handout and crayons.)

Give each child crayons and a handout. Read the words. Ask kids to say them with you as you read them again: **God wants us to share**. Explain that the bread in the picture represents the bread the widow shared with Elijah in the Bible story.

Let children color their bread shapes. SAY: **You've really learned your lesson well because I see several of you sharing your crayons.**

Have kids share their art by exchanging with someone else.

7. I Love to Share

Ask kids to stand and join hands in a circle. Sing the following song to the tune of "Twinkle, Twinkle, Little Star." Go through the song slowly and teach the words and actions. Repeat it several times.

How I, how I love to share (walk to the middle of the circle)

With my neighbors everywhere. (Walk out.)

It pleases Jesus when I do. (Kids point up.)

It makes us happy, me and you. (Kids shake hands with someone and join hands in a circle again.)

How I, how I love to share (walk to the middle of the circle)

With my neighbors everywhere. (Walk out.)

8. Share Prayer

(You'll need the modeling dough and sandwich bags.)

Ask children to stay in the circle, holding hands. PRAY: **Dear God, thank you for your gifts. Help us share what we have with others. Amen.**

Give each child a handful of the modeling dough in a sandwich bag to take home and share with someone.

by Ray and Cindy Peppers

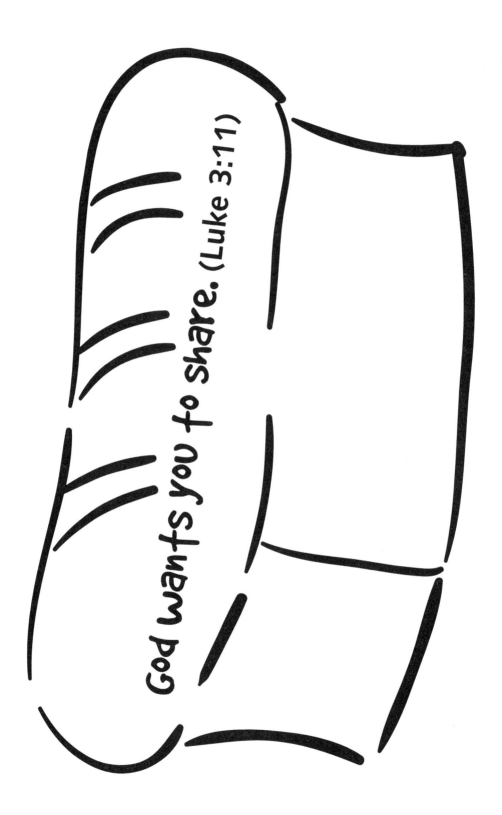

God wants you to share. (Luke 3:11)

Don't Fight!

A Powerful Purpose

Preschool children will learn to be peacemakers instead of fighters.

A Look at the Lesson

1. Be a Friend . . . . (up to 6 minutes)
2. It's Mine . . . . (up to 6 minutes)
3. Jesus Tells Us . . . . (up to 4 minutes)
4. Act Out a Story . . . . (up to 6 minutes)
5. Puppet Productions . . . . (up to 8 minutes)
6. Puppet Performance . . . . (up to 8 minutes)
7. A Snack Like David's . . . . (up to 5 minutes)
8. Blessed Are the Peacemakers . . . . (up to 4 minutes)

Many of today's TV shows and movies teach that the one who's strongest is best. The person who gets in the last "hit" is the winner. But Jesus says to turn the other cheek. He says if someone wants your shirt, give him your coat, too. Again and again we see Jesus making peace among would-be fighters.

Use this lesson to help young children learn more about being peacemakers instead of fighters. God wants us to bring peace, not harm, to others.

THE LIVELY LESSON

1. Be a Friend

As kids enter the room, gather them in a line for an opening game. With one of the taller kids, form a "bridge": Face each other, grab each other's hands, and hold them up high in an arch. Ask children to travel under the bridge, around you, and back under the bridge while you sing this song to the tune of "London Bridge":

A SPRINKLING OF SUPPLIES

- ❏ Bible
- ❏ crayons
- ❏ paper plates
- ❏ craft sticks
- ❏ tape
- ❏ tables
- ❏ fresh fruit
- ❏ water
- ❏ cups
- ❏ napkins

Friends are always, always kind,
Always kind,
Always kind,
Friends are always, always kind,
Be a friend, [Name].

On the words "Be a friend, [Name]," say the child's name who's under the bridge at that time, and bring your clasped arms down around him or her. Gently rock the child back and forth as you sing:

Never, never hurt others,
Hurt others,
Hurt others,
Never, never hurt others,
Be a friend, [Name].

Now let the person you just rocked switch places with the person who was helping you form a bridge. Continue until everyone gets a turn being rocked. Encourage all kids to sing with you.

2. It's Mine

(You'll need one crayon for every two people. You'll also need a Bible.)

SAY: **We're going to talk about fighting and hurting each other. We're going to discover better, peaceful ways to solve problems instead of hurtful ways of doing it.**

Form pairs. Give every pair a crayon and ask the partners to both hold it. On the count of three, have them pretend to fight over the crayon. One says, "It's mine," and pulls it toward himself; the other says, "No! It's mine," and pulls it toward herself. Have them keep going back and forth like this until you say "stop."

After children have pretended awhile, tell them to stop, then ASK:

• How did it feel to fight over a crayon?

• Have you fought over toys or clothes or food before? When?

• Instead of fighting over the crayon,

how could we solve the problem?

SAY: **One way to solve that kind of problem is to share. Take turns. Jesus wants us to think of others and help them. Listen to his advice.**

Read Luke 6:29: "If someone strikes you on one cheek, turn to him the other also. If someone takes your cloak, do not stop him from taking your tunic."

In other words, don't fight.

ASK: **What are some things that make you so mad that you want to fight?** Listen for things such as bullies, people not sharing toys, hitting, not playing fair.

Ask children about ways to handle the situations. Help them think of positive reactions.

3. Jesus Tells Us

Sing this song to the tune of "Mary Had a Little Lamb." Sing through the two verses several times to help kids learn it.

If a person makes you mad,
Makes you mad,
Makes you mad,
If a person makes you mad,
Turn the other cheek.

Jesus tells us do not fight,
Do not fight,
Do not fight,
Jesus tells us do not fight,
Be a peacemaker.

Tell kids that a peacemaker is someone who loves other people and doesn't fight.

4. Act Out a Story

SAY: **We're going to hear a Bible story about David and King Saul. David had a chance to fight, but he didn't. I'll say some words and do some actions, you repeat the words and the actions.**

This story is from 1 Samuel 26.

Saul was a king. *(Stand proud.)*

David was a brave young man. *(Arm across chest, look brave.)*

King Saul was jealous and wanted to kill David. *(Look jealous.)*

David feared for his life, so he ran. *(Run in place.)*

King Saul went looking for David. *(Hand above eyes and look.)*

One night while King Saul was sleeping *(fold hands by cheek, close eyes, and say, "Z-z-z-z-z-z-z"),*

David quietly came up to him. *(Tiptoe in place, put finger to lips, and say, "Sh-h-h-h-h-h.")*

David could have killed King Saul. *(Raise arm as if you're going to strike.)*

But he didn't. *(Drop arm and shake head.)*

He took Saul's spear and water jug *(pretend to lift one in each hand)*

And left. *(Tiptoe quietly.)*

He then yelled at the king's guard away at a safe distance, "Wake up!" *(Cup hands around mouth and yell words.)*

"You weren't doing your job!" *(Say the words loudly.)*

"I could have killed King Saul!" *(Say the words loudly.)*

"But I didn't!" *(Say the words loudly.)*

David threw down King Saul's spear and water jug to prove it. *(Pretend to throw down each item.)*

King Saul heard this *(hand to ear)*

And said, "May you be blessed, David." *(Say the words loudly.)*

"God is with you." *(Point up.)*

And King Saul went back home. *(Walk in place.)*

SAY: **David could have fought, but he didn't.**

5. Puppet Productions

(Make puppets by taping a craft stick handle on the back of each paper plate. Make two for each child. You'll also need crayons.)

SAY: **Now we're going to make puppets and perform David's story again.**

Give each child two paper plate puppets and crayons. Tell kids to design a David puppet and a King Saul puppet. You design a couple puppets along with them so they can see examples.

6. Puppet Performance

(You'll need the completed puppets and a puppet stage. Make a stage by turning a table on its side. Use as many tables as you can so half the class can perform at a time.)

SAY: **Hold up your King Saul puppets. They look great! Everybody say, "Hi, King Saul!" Now hold up your David puppets. They look great too! Everybody say, "Hi, David!"**

Have half of the class find a place behind the puppet stage; the other half of the class will be the audience. SAY: **Lights! Cameras! Action!** Read the story again, only this time have the puppets perform.

Then switch and let the other half of the class perform while the others watch.

7. A Snack Like David's

(You'll need fresh fruit, water, cups, and napkins.)

Ask kids what they think David might have eaten while he was running from Saul. He had to live in the desert and in the mountains. Some suggestions are wild game, nuts, seeds, berries, and lots of water for his thirst. Serve children fresh fruit and water.

SAY: **David couldn't be at his house eating home-cooked meals while Saul was chasing him, so he had to eat a lot of these other things. David must have thanked God even for what he had. Let's thank God for these snacks and for David, who showed us not to fight. There are better ways to solve problems.**

Pray as a group. Have kids repeat each line after you:

Come, Lord Jesus,
Help us find
Ways that are peaceful,
Thoughtful, kind.
When we feel
We want to fight,
Help us stop
With your power and might.
Amen.

8. Blessed Are the Peacemakers

(Teach Matthew 5:9 as the memory verse. Sing the following words to the tune of "Jesus Loves Me.")

Blessed are the peacemakers,
Blessed are the peacemakers,
Blessed are the peacemakers,
Blessed are the peacemakers.

Let's be peacemakers,
Let's be peacemakers,
Let's be peacemakers,
And do what God would do.

Let children take their puppets home and perform the David and Saul story for their families.

by Ray and Cindy Peppers

Lend a Helping Hand

A Powerful Purpose

Preschool children will hear a Bible story about the good Samaritan and practice helping others.

A Look at the Lesson

Preschool children love to help. They enjoy getting along with others and want to please. Helping other people encourages interaction, reinforces biblical values, and helps model Christian behavior.

Use this lesson to teach preschoolers about helping. Give them a chance to be kind to each other.

THE LIVELY LESSON

1. Fast First Aid

(Place the following supplies on a table: a doll, adhesive bandages, wet washcloths, towels.)

Welcome children and tell them they're going to learn about helping others. Gather around the table with the doll and first-aid supplies on it. SAY: **Pretend this doll is a little child and she's just been hurt. What could you use to help her feel better?**

Let children wipe the doll with wet washcloths, dry her off, and put on adhesive bandages. Then ASK:

A SPRINKLING OF SUPPLIES

- ❏ doll
- ❏ adhesive bandages
- ❏ wet washcloths
- ❏ towels
- ❏ Bible
- ❏ photocopies of the handout (p. 44)
- ❏ napkins
- ❏ cups
- ❏ milk
- ❏ marker
- ❏ envelopes
- ❏ postage stamps
- ❏ cookies
- ❏ crayons

- How did we help this doll?
- Have you ever helped someone? When?
- How does it make you feel when you help someone?

2. The Good Samaritan

(You'll need a Bible.)

SAY: **Jesus told stories of how other people were helpers too. Let's read about a helper called the good Samaritan. He was a man from a country called Samaria.**

Read the story from Luke 10:30-37 in a children's Bible. Pause after each verse. Have kids say, "Jesus wants us to help" and clap as they say each word.

Then retell the story and have the children act out the different parts as you tell it. Be sure each child has a part, whether as an actor or as a part of the scenery.

3. Create a Card

(Photocopy the "Create a Card" handout and provide crayons. Ask your pastor about congregation members who are ill or who need extra prayers and encouragement. Make a list of their names and addresses.)

SAY: **Today we're going to be God's helpers too. We're going to help people feel better. We're going to make get-well cards for people who are sick or need some cheering up.**

Give each child a handout and crayons. Read the words: **God loves you so much. He's watching over you.** Fold the cards with the words inside. Have kids decorate the blank outsides of the cards and color the picture on the inside.

4. Repeat-After-Me Prayer

Ask kids to pray by repeating each line you say and the actions you do.

Dear God (fold hands),

We are your helpers. (Raise hands to heaven.)

Let us be good helpers this week (put hands on shoulders)

To all of those people around us. (Motion arms all around.)

Amen. (Fold hands.)

5. Cookie Snack

(You'll need napkins, cups, milk, and cookies.)

Follow the prayer with a snack of milk and cookies. As they munch on their cookies, let children look at the card designs others made.

6. Bandage Reminder

(You'll need adhesive bandages and a marker.)

Gather kids in a circle and ask:

- Who are God's helpers? (Name each child in the class.)
- How do we help others?

To help remind them of today's lesson and the fact that they are God's helpers, write, "Luke 10:30-37" on an adhesive bandage for each child. Place the bandages on the backs of kids' hands.

Tell kids that Luke 10:30-37 is the place in the Bible that tells about God's helper, the good Samaritan. Encourage kids to ask a parent to read the story again at home.

7. Mail a Card

(You'll need envelopes, addresses of those to receive cards, and postage stamps. Mark an X on each envelope where kids are to stick a stamp.)

Let kids place their cards in envelopes and place stamps in the corners over the X. Let them take their cards home to mail. Or, if time allows, take the entire class to a nearby mailbox and let kids mail their cards.

by Nanette Goings

Create a Card

God loves you so much. He's watching over you.

How Do You Feel?

A Powerful Purpose

Preschool children will learn to use words to tell family and friends how they feel.

A Look at the Lesson

A SPRINKLING OF SUPPLIES

- ❏ Bible
- ❏ marker
- ❏ old shirts or smocks
- ❏ magazines
- ❏ cookie dough
- ❏ raisins
- ❏ sandwich bags
- ❏ wax paper
- ❏ shaving cream
- ❏ paper plates
- ❏ CD of lively music
- ❏ CD player
- ❏ sandpaper
- ❏ red yarn
- ❏ crayons
- ❏ scarf for each child
- ❏ photocopies of handout (p. 49)
- ❏ water
- ❏ towels

Young children aren't yet equipped with appropriate outlets for emotions and often express them in negative ways. They're confused by reactions around them and are searching for a way to help others understand how they feel.

It's OK to feel happy, sad, angry, lonely, and scared. God knows how children feel and can help them deal with their emotions. But other people around them need to know about those emotions as well. If children hit, scream, or cry, others may not understand. But if children learn to use words to express their feelings, others will better be able to help.

Use this lesson to give children opportunities to explore their emotions and express them to others.

THE LIVELY LESSON

1. If You're Happy

Welcome the children, then lead them in singing the traditional song "If You're Happy and You Know It."

After the song, gather the children in front of you and teach this action poem:

Sometimes I feel happy. (Show happy face.)

Sometimes I feel sad. (Show sad face.)

Sometimes I feel sleepy. (Yawn.)

And sometimes I feel mad. (Show angry face.)

But no matter how I'm feeling (shrug shoulders),

God helps me to be strong (show muscles)

And to tell about my feelings (point to mouth)

All day long. (Clap on each word.)

SAY: **God made you with all kinds of feelings inside. It's OK to feel happy, sad, scared, lonely, and even mad. But God wants us to share our feelings and not keep them locked up inside. We know he'll help us understand how we feel and give us the words to tell others too. He tells us in the Bible that he'll be there to help us when we need him. He can help us not feel sad, scared, lonely, or mad when we trust him to take care of us.**

Read Hebrews 13:6b: "The Lord is my helper; I will not be afraid."

SAY: **Because the Lord is our helper, he'll help us get rid of the feelings that bother us if we tell him about them.**

2. Guess the Feelings

(Clip pictures from magazines that show people expressing diverse emotions such as fear, anger, happiness, and worry.)

Show the magazine pictures to the children and ask:

• **What do you see in this picture?**

• **What do you think is happening in this picture?**

• **How do you think this person feels?**

• **How do you know the person feels this way?**

• **Have you ever felt this way? When?**

Throughout the discussion, emphasize that other people share the same emotions the children do. God knows how we feel, and other people will understand our feelings too.

Throughout the discussion, encourage language such as, "I feel angry when ..." or "I feel sad when ..." This way, the children can practice verbalizing their feelings within a safe environment.

3. Cookie Faces

(Provide sliced refrigerator cookie dough and raisins.)

Give children each two slices of cookie dough. Encourage them to use the raisins to make a face on each cookie. Direct them to make their cookie faces each express a feeling.

Ask kids to tell the feeling they're giving each of their two cookies. While you continue with the lesson, have an adult helper bake the cookies.

Note: If you don't have access to an oven, let the children decorate prepared cookies that have frosting on them.

4. Finger Painting Feelings

(You'll need wax paper, shaving cream, and old shirts or aprons.)

Cover kids' good clothes with old shirts or smocks. Give kids each a large piece of wax paper, and have them sit at the table. On each piece of wax paper, place a small mound of shaving cream. Encourage the children to use their fingers and hands to spread the cream out on the paper.

Invite children to draw faces showing

different emotions. SAY: **Draw how you feel when**

- **someone gives you a candy bar.**
- **someone sneaks up behind you and yells, "Boo!"**
- **you trip and fall down, scraping your knee on the sidewalk.**

Encourage children to continue drawing other emotions and talking about the situations. Remind them that God knows how they feel and that they can tell others too.

Use water and towels to clean up in the room, or take children to a restroom.

5. March Around the Feelings

(On paper plates draw various faces depicting a variety of feelings. Make several of each kind so you'll have one for each child. You'll also need a CD of lively music and a CD player.)

Place the paper plate faces in a circle on the floor. SAY: **Look at all the paper faces on the floor. They show all kinds of feelings such as happiness, sadness, and anger. I'll play some music, and you march around outside the circle of faces. When the music stops, you stop. Look at the plate in front of you and pretend to feel that way. Then we'll talk about that feeling.**

Continue the game, playing music and stopping until everyone has had an opportunity to talk about several feelings.

6. Feel the Feelings

(Each child will need a scarf or piece of silky material. Chiffon scarves work best and can be found at second-hand stores.)

Give children each a scarf or piece of silky material. Tell them to practice twirling their scarves all around them in a happy way and quietly repeat the phrase, "Sometimes I feel happy, happy, happy." Then, tell them to stop, pretend to be angry, and wad the scarf into a ball. Direct them to throw the scarf into the air as they repeat the phrase, "Sometimes I feel angry, angry, angry." They can catch the scarves and try again until you direct them to resume moving in a happy way.

Alternate feelings and actions as time and interest permit. Remember to repeat the phrases so children can hear how to verbalize these feelings.

SAY: **See how easy it is to talk about feelings? We need to remember to let God and others know how we feel.**

7. Sandpaper Faces

(Each child will need crayons, a 3-inch piece of red yarn, and a 5-inch circle that has been cut from sandpaper.)

Give each child a sandpaper circle. Direct them to use crayons to make eyes and a nose. Give each child a 3-inch piece of red yarn to be used as a mouth. The yarn will stick to the sandpaper and can be changed from a smile to a frown to an angry face.

Give children an opportunity to decide which emotion they want their sandpaper faces to display and to show them to others. Let children tell about times they experienced those emotions. Praise them for their efforts, and remind them how important it is to tell God and others how they feel when they experience similar situations.

8. Lip-Smacking Snack Time

(You'll need the baked cookies, sandwich bags, and photocopies of the handout.)

Let kids each eat one cookie they made. Talk about the feelings depicted.

Close by paraphrasing Hebrews 13:6: **[Name] will not be afraid because the Lord is [Name]'s helper.** Say this to each child, using his or her name.

SAY: **When we tell God about our fears or our other feelings, he'll help us handle them in a good way.**

Let kids take home their other cookies in sandwich bags. Attach the "Cookie Face" handout. Write each child's name in the blanks provided on the handout.

Read the note aloud to kids: **Hi! I'm a cookie face. [Name] made me. Ask [Name] to tell you how I feel.**

SAY: **Be sure you tell your family what kind of face and feeling you designed for your cookie. Remember that God is your helper. He'll help you handle all your feelings in a good way.**

by Jane P. Wilke

Cookie Face

Hi! I'm a cookie face.

_____ made me.

Ask _____ to tell

you how I feel.

Caring for God's World

A Powerful Purpose

Preschool children will learn practical ways to care for God's creation.

A Look at the Lesson

C hildren this age are naturally enthusiastic about the world around them. Animals, trees, colors, shapes, smells—everything in nature is a source of great delight.

Use this lesson as an adventure for all of the senses. Focus the children's attention on how things feel (the sun on their faces), smell (flowers), taste (things to eat), sound (birds and animals), and look (all creation around them). Use this time to help children discover the wonders of God's world and to recognize how sad we would be if we were to lose any of it.

A SPRINKLING OF SUPPLIES

- ❒ Bible
- ❒ simple puzzles with nature or animal pictures on them
- ❒ magazines
- ❒ newsprint
- ❒ tape
- ❒ safety pins
- ❒ crayons
- ❒ O-shaped cereal
- ❒ yarn
- ❒ fruit
- ❒ photocopies of the handouts (pp. 53-54)

THE LIVELY LESSON

1. Puzzles—Putting It Together

(You'll need several simple puzzles with nature or animal pictures on them.)

Place the puzzles around on the floor. As children enter the room, invite them to put the puzzles together. Encourage kids to work together and cooperate to complete the pictures. As children work, talk with them about the pictures and other things God has created.

2. Experience God's Creation

(Do this activity outdoors. In case of bad weather, prepare an indoor nature walk. Tape pictures of flowers, sun, streams, and animals on walls in the hall or various rooms.)

SAY: **Today we're going to take a nature walk and experience all of God's creation. We're going to see** (point to your eyes and have kids point to their eyes), **hear** (point to your ears and have kids point to their ears), **smell** (point to your nose and have kids each point to their noses), **taste** (point to your mouth and have kids point to their mouths), **and feel** (wiggle your fingers and have kids wiggle their fingers) **God's wonderful creation.**

Go outside and:

• See the clouds, sun, trees, and seasonal gifts such as flowers.

• Hear the birds, insects, and wind.

• Smell the flowers, and trees.

• Taste a gulp of fresh air.

• Feel rough tree bark, smooth rocks, and the cool grass beneath your feet.

3. Let's Make a World

(Draw a large circle on a piece of newsprint, and tape it to the wall. You'll also need magazines.)

When you come back to the room, distribute the magazines. Ask children what they liked best about the nature walk. Ask them to find pictures of what they liked and tear them out. SAY: **Remember everything you saw, heard, smelled, tasted, and felt.**

SAY: **Our world is a beautiful place. God created it with all kinds of wonderful things! Let's make a picture of our world and put on it all the things we liked from our walk.**

Ask children to bring up the items they tore out and lightly tape them in the circle. Try to include a wide variety of pictures. When you've finished, stand back, look at the world, and have everyone say, "What a wonderful world!"

4. Something's Missing

SAY: **God made the things we've put into our world. What would our world be like without them?**

Start taking photos off, one by one. After removing each one, ask children: **How would you feel if [flowers, clouds, animals, water] weren't in our world anymore?**

When you've taken everything off, ASK: **If all of these wonderful gifts were gone, what would the world be like?**

Listen to children's responses such as empty, ugly, wouldn't smell as good.

5. Care Walk

(You'll need photocopies of the "What Can I Do?" handout.)

Read Genesis 1:26: **"Then God said, 'Let us make man in our image, in our likeness, and let them rule over the fish of the sea and the birds of the air, over the livestock, over all the earth, and over all the creatures that move along the ground.' "** Like a parent takes care of a child he or she **"rules over,"** we need to take care of our world.

After you read from the Bible, have kids stand and say, "Let's take care of God's creation!"

SAY: **There are some simple things we can do to help take care of our earth. Follow me and I'll show you.**

Take children on a walking tour to show the ideas on the "What Can I Do?" handout. For example, lead kids to a light switch and read: **Turn off the lights when you leave a room.** Lead them to a water faucet and read: **Don't run the water when brushing your teeth.**

After your Care Walk, return to the room. Give each child a photocopy of the "What Can I Do?" handout. SAY: **Take this list home and show it to your mom or dad. Ask your mom or dad to help you do at least one of these things during the next week.**

6. Earth Patrol

(You'll need photocopies of the "God's Earth Patrol" handout. Cut out the badges. You'll also need safety pins and crayons.)

Give each child a badge and crayons. Read the words: **"God's Earth Patrol."** Let children color the badges. When you pin a finished badge to each child, SAY: **I now commission you to God's Earth Patrol. It's your job to keep watch and take care of the earth.**

After everyone has been commissioned,

PRAY: **Father, thank you for this wonderful, beautiful world you have given us. Help us not to hurt it anymore. Help us learn how to take care of it. Amen.**

7. Bird Feeders

(You'll need O-shaped cereal, such as Cheerios, and 10-inch pieces of yarn.)

SAY: **One thing we all can do is help take care of the wild animals that live near us. We're going to make bird feeders that can be hung from a tree branch or out a window. When birds come to visit your house, they'll have something good to eat!**

Give each child a length of yarn and a handful of cereal. Help each child tie a knot at the end of his or her yarn, then let children thread the cereal onto the yarn. You may want to put a small piece of tape at the end of the yarn to prevent it from fraying as children thread the cereal.

As children finish, help them tie the ends of the yarn so the cereal stays in place, then serve the children a snack of fruit.

by Karen M. Ball

What Can I Do?

1. Turn off the lights when you leave a room.

2. Don't run the water when brushing your teeth. Just turn it on to wet your brush and to rinse it off.

3. Put a plastic jug filled with water in your toilet's tank so it doesn't use as much water.

4. Use a cloth towel instead of a paper towel to dry your hands.

5. Paint and draw on recycled paper.

6. Set dry bread out in your yard for the birds to eat.

7. Throw trash in trash cans, not on the ground.

8. Recycle! Newspapers, cans, bottles, plastic, cereal boxes, aluminum foil—all can be recycled.

9. Pick up litter when you see it.

10. Cut the plastic rings that come on six-packs before you throw them in the trash. Small animals foraging through local dump sites have caught their necks in the rings.

11. Check with your local zoo to see if they have an adopt-an-animal program. Help care for all of God's creation.

God's Earth Patrol

God's Earth Patrol

Part 3: A Lively Look at My Faith

Who Is God?

A Powerful Purpose

Preschool children will learn about God and how much he loves them.

A Look at the Lesson

Preschoolers are beginning to form their ideas about who God is. Some view God as a loving parent. Others think of him as a grandfather-type. And others think of him as one who doesn't like them to do certain things.

Preschoolers need their questions about God answered simply and truthfully. Use this lesson to help your preschoolers learn about God and how he loved us so much he sent us his Son, Jesus.

A SPRINKLING OF SUPPLIES

- ❏ crayons
- ❏ red construction paper
- ❏ glue sticks
- ❏ Bible
- ❏ animal crackers
- ❏ milk
- ❏ cups
- ❏ photocopies of the handouts (pp. 59-60)

THE LIVELY LESSON

1. Color Their World

(For each child, you'll need crayons and a photocopy of the "God Made the World" handout.)

Welcome the children as they arrive. Give them each a photocopy of the "God Made the World" handout and crayons. Have them color the items on the page.

After everyone has had a chance to color, ASK:

• **Who made the things you just colored?**
• **Why did God make them?**

SAY: **We know God loves us, and one of the reasons we know that is that he made wonderful flowers, trees, and animals and gave them to us to enjoy.**

2. The Bible Tells Me So

SAY: **Another reason we know God loves us is because the Bible tells us that he does.**

Help kids memorize this Bible verse: "Love comes from God" (1 John 4:7). Use motions to convey the words to the children as you say them.

Love *(wrap your arms around yourself)*
Comes *(motion with your hand as if signaling someone to come to you)*
From God. *(Point up.)*

Say the verse with the children three or four times. Have them stand and do the motions with you. Then let the children try saying one word by themselves as you do the motions. After a couple more times, they should be able to say the verse by themselves.

3. Jesus Loves Me

SAY: **The Bible tells us that love comes from God. The Bible also tells us that Jesus loves us.**

Sing "Jesus Loves Me" with the children. Use these actions.

Jesus *(point up)*
Loves *(wrap arms around yourself)*
Me *(point to yourself)*;
This I know *(point to your head)*,
For the Bible *(form a Bible with your two hands)*

Tells me so. *(Point to yourself.)*
Little ones *(motion like your hand is placed on a little child's head)*
To him belong. *(Point up.)*
They are weak *(look weak)*,
But he is strong. *(Form strong arms.)*

Yes *(nod head)*,
Jesus *(point up)*
Loves *(wrap arms around yourself)*
Me. *(Point to yourself.)*
(Repeat "Yes, Jesus loves me" three times.)
The Bible *(form a Bible with your two hands)*
Tells me so. *(Point to yourself.)*

SAY: **To remind us that God loves us, too, let's put his name in place of Jesus' name in the song.**

Sing "God Loves Me" using the same actions.

4. Hugs of Love

(You'll need a Bible.)

SAY: **You know what? I love you too!** Go around and hug each child as you call him or her by name and SAY: **[Name], I love you.** Have kids move to a different part of the room and sit down on the floor. Then SAY: **I hugged you to show my love for you. God doesn't come and hug us like I hugged you. But he has shown us how much he loves us by sending us his Son, Jesus.**

Read a children's Bible version of John 3:16, or read this: **"For God loved the world so much that he gave his only Son. God gave his Son so that whoever believes in him may not be lost, but have eternal life."**

5. He Gave Us Us

SAY: **Another way God shows us he loves us is by giving us bodies that do things. Let's stand up and thank God for the bodies he has given us.**

Have kids spread out. Tell them to repeat the words after you and follow your motions. Be sensitive to special needs children in your class. Adapt any motions they can't do so that everyone can participate.

Thanks, God, for our hands. (*Wave hands in the air.*)

Thanks, God, for our feet. (*Wiggle a foot in the air.*)

Thanks, God, for our elbows. (*Flop your elbows out at your sides.*)

Thanks, God, for our knees. (*March with your knees going high.*)

Thanks, God, for our heads. (*Roll your head around and around.*)

Thanks, God, for our hips. (*Wiggle your hips.*)

Thanks, God, for our seats. (*Sit down on the floor in a circle.*)

6. Animals for Us

(You'll need animal crackers, milk, and cups.)

Distribute the animal crackers and serve the milk. Before letting kids eat their crackers, go around the circle and let them describe one of their animals. SAY: **Remember what we colored earlier? God loves us so much he gave us all sorts of neat things in our world. Some of those things are animals. And the milk we're drinking came from one of those animals: a cow!**

Offer a prayer thanking God for the love he showed us by giving us animals.

7. A Heart for God

(You'll need glue sticks, crayons, red hearts cut from construction paper, and the "God Loves Me" handouts. Cut the hearts so they fit over the heart shape on the handout.)

Distribute the handouts, glue sticks, and red paper hearts. Read the handout and explain where to glue the hearts. Let the children glue the hearts in place and color the letters.

Ask if anyone remembers the memory verse (Love comes from God). If no one says it, say it with the children a couple more times. Work through it until they can say it with you, doing the motions.

8. Love Prayer

(You'll need the completed "God Loves Me" handouts.)

Place the "God Loves Me" handouts in the center of the room. Ask the children to form a circle around the handouts. SAY: **Look at all of these reminders of God's love. Let's pray and thank God for his love.**

Pray, thanking God for showing us his love in so many ways—God's Son, ourselves, animals, and our world.

Then have kids place their arms on each other's shoulders and take three steps in toward the center. When they're all bunched together in a group hug, have everybody shout, "God loves us!"

by Paul Woods

God Made the World

Who Is Jesus?

A Powerful Purpose

*Preschool children will learn that
Jesus is their friend. He's with them all the time.*

A Look at the Lesson

1. Jesus Is With Me . . . . (up to 6 minutes)
2. Crayon Resist . . . . (up to 6 minutes)
3. Shadow Screen . . . . (up to 5 minutes)
4. Listen and Do . . . . (up to 3 minutes)
5. Follow the Leader . . . . (up to 6 minutes)
6. Door Hanger Design . . . . (up to 8 minutes)
7. Jesus Hugs . . . . (up to 5 minutes)
8. Picture Pass Around . . . . (up to 5 minutes)

A SPRINKLING OF SUPPLIES

- ☐ Bible
- ☐ white crayons
- ☐ white construction paper
- ☐ watercolors
- ☐ different colors of tissue paper
- ☐ glue sticks
- ☐ crayons
- ☐ paintbrushes
- ☐ old shirts or smocks
- ☐ photocopies of the handout (p. 64)
- ☐ slide or overhead projector
- ☐ piece of thin white cloth
- ☐ objects for the shadow screen
- ☐ picture of Jesus
- ☐ twisted pretzels
- ☐ apple juice
- ☐ napkins
- ☐ cups

Young children think in a concrete manner and, therefore, it's difficult for them to understand abstract concepts. They're told that Jesus loves them; however, they can't see him. To help young children understand this abstract concept, we must help them make a connection with concrete activities.

Use this lesson to repeat the theme "Jesus is with me wherever I go." Activities reiterate the theme as well as reinforce the concept.

THE LIVELY LESSON

1. Jesus Is With Me

(You'll need a Bible.)
Gather children in a circle. Lead them in this action song to the tune of "The Mulberry Bush."

**This is the way we swing our arms,
Swing our arms, swing our arms.**

This is the way we swing our arms
In praise to the Lord.

Sing other verses and actions such as nod our heads, clap our hands, wiggle our fingers, and march in place.

After several verses, change the song's words. Do the actions in place.

Jesus is with me when I run,
When I run, when I run.
Jesus is with me when I run;
He's with me wherever I go.

Sing other verses and actions such as when I walk, jump, skate, stretch, sleep, throw, and eat.

End the activity by singing "Jesus is with me when I sit..." After kids sit, open your Bible to Matthew 28:20. Tell kids to listen quietly as you read what Jesus said: **"I am with you always."**

Remind kids of the song, and talk briefly about the variety of times Jesus is with them throughout both day and night.

2. Crayon Resist

(You'll need a white crayon and white piece of construction paper for each child. You'll also need watercolors, paintbrushes, and old shirts or smocks.)

Cover kids' good clothes with old shirts or smocks. Give each child a white crayon and a piece of white construction paper. Instruct kids to draw a scribble design all over the paper, pressing hard with the crayon. Talk with them about how difficult it is to see the design. Then let kids paint over the entire surface of the paper with watercolors. The design will appear on the page as the crayon wax resists the paint. Share with kids that Jesus is also with us even though we can't see him.

3. Shadow Screen

(Gather a variety of objects recognizable by shape, such as a rock, pencil, cup, and fork. Place them in a bag or a box. Add a cutout shape of Jesus. Then construct a simple shadow screen by hanging a thin white cloth in front of a beam of light from a slide or overhead projector. Nail the cloth to a wooden frame or drape it over a table.)

Set children in front of the shadow screen. Place one of the objects in the beam of light, behind the cloth. Ask kids to guess what it is by looking at the shadow. Follow this procedure with all of the shapes, and end with the cutout shape of Jesus. SAY: **Just like we knew what all the other shapes were, we also knew Jesus. Jesus is with us even though we can't see him.**

If kids don't recognize Jesus, SAY: **Even though we didn't recognize Jesus like the other things, he's always there.**

4. Listen and Do

Ask children to find a place on the floor, kneel down, touch their chins to their chests, and cover their closed eyes with their hands. Tiptoe quietly to a spot and SAY:

Peanut butter and strawberry jam,
Can you point to where I am?

Ask kids to keep their eyes closed and point to you. Tiptoe to a new location and repeat the activity several times. When finished, reinforce that the children knew you were there even though they couldn't see you, just like we know Jesus is here even though we can't see him.

5. Follow the Leader

Gather children in a circle. Walk around them as you sing the following song to the tune of "The Farmer in the Dell."

Jesus loves me so.
Yes, Jesus loves me so.
He is with me day and night,
Wherever I may go.

As you finish, tap a child on the head and ask him or her to follow you around the circle. Encourage the children to sing with you and continue until everyone is following you.

Keep singing the verse and begin to lead the group around the room. Add an action they can do while singing. For example, tap head, twirl slowly, or clap hands above head. At the end of the verse, go to the back of the line and direct the child in front to lead with an action. Continue with the activity until everyone has had an opportunity to lead.

If a child hesitates to lead, invite him or her to come join you, and continue with the next person.

Conclude the activity by gathering in a circle, holding hands, singing the verse, and adding a jump and a "Hey!" at the end.

6. Door Hanger Design

(Photocopy the "Door Hanger" handout, one for each child. Photocopy them onto heavy paper. Provide crayons, small pieces of different colors of tissue paper, and glue sticks.)

Give each child a "Door Hanger" handout. Read the words on it: **"Jesus is with me!"** Let children decorate the hangers with crayons and by gluing crumpled tissue paper on them.

7. Jesus Hugs

(You'll need twisted pretzels, apple juice, napkins, and cups.)

Serve pretzels and juice as the snack.

Have children look at the pretzels and notice the cross pattern. Have them cross their arms in front of their chests in the same manner. Call this a "Jesus Hug." Say that even though we can't see Jesus, we can still feel his presence and pretend to feel his hugs. With their arms crossed, lead children in this prayer: **Thank you, Jesus, for loving us and being with us wherever we go. Thank you for the food to make our bodies strong. Help us to feel your hugs every day. Amen.**

8. Picture Pass Around

(You'll need a picture of Jesus.)

Gather in a circle once more. Repeat Matthew 28:20: "I am with you always." Show children the picture of Jesus, then SAY: **Pictures of Jesus remind us that he is with us wherever we go.**

Pass the picture around the circle. As each child holds the picture, have him or her complete the sentence "Jesus is with me when I _____."

Accept each answer even if it's repeated. Answers may include sleep, run, jump, talk, eat, cry.

When the picture returns to you, sum up all the responses as you lead children in the following reading. Fill in the blank with one of the kids' words and repeat until all the responses have been included.

Teacher: **For being with us when we _____ ,**

Children: Thank you, Jesus.

Encourage kids to take home their door hangers. Ask kids to hang them on their bedroom door knobs as reminders that Jesus is with them always.

by Jane P. Wilke

Door Hanger

Jesus is with me!

Talking to God

A Powerful Purpose

Preschool children will understand what prayer is and that God hears their prayers.

A Look at the Lesson

1. What Is Prayer? . . . . (up to 4 minutes)
2. God Answers Prayer . . . . (up to 6 minutes)
3. Fishy Snack. (up to 6 minutes)
4. Prayer Topics . . . . (up to 6 minutes)
5. Prayer Bracelets . . . . (up to 6 minutes)
6. Pray Always . . . . (up to 3 minutes)
7. God Listens. (up to 4 minutes)
8. Time to Pray. . . . . (up to 3 minutes)
9. Thank You, God . . . . (up to 3 minutes)

Many young children love to pray, but they have lots of questions about how prayer works. They need to know that prayer is one way to talk to God. God hears our prayers, and God answers our prayers.

Use this lesson to teach children more about prayer—a way to talk to God.

A SPRINKLING OF SUPPLIES

- ❏ Bible
- ❏ photocopies of the handouts (pp. 68-71)
- ❏ puppets
- ❏ table
- ❏ basket
- ❏ fish-shaped crackers
- ❏ juice
- ❏ cups
- ❏ napkins
- ❏ crayons
- ❏ safety scissors
- ❏ hole punch
- ❏ yarn

THE LIVELY LESSON

1. What Is Prayer?

(Use puppets or actors to perform the "What Is Prayer?" skit. Turn a table on its side to use as a puppet stage.)

Welcome the children into the room and ask them to sit down. SAY: **Let's listen to these two people and see what we're going to learn today.**

When the puppets finish, have the children show their appreciation by giving them a standing ovation. Stand and clap and cheer!

2. God Answers Prayer

(You'll need a Bible, a basket, and cutout fish and loaves from photocopies of the "Fish and Loaves" handout.)

Read about Jesus feeding a crowd of people in Matthew 14:13-21. Then tell children they're going to act out the story.

Ask one of the older children to be Jesus. Give this child a basket with the cutout fish and loaves in the bottom. You'll need enough fish and loaves to distribute to each child and still have some left over. Don't allow the other children to see in the bottom of the basket.

Choose two or three others to be disciples. Give them cutouts of five loaves of bread and two fish.

Everyone else plays the hungry crowd.

Narrate the story and help children act out their parts.

Jesus saw a huge crowd of people and felt sorry for them. *(Jesus looks around at the crowd of people.)*

It was late in the day, and they were hungry. *(Kids rub their tummies and moan, "We're hungry.")*

The disciples came to Jesus. *(Walk toward Jesus.)*

They said, "We can't feed them. We only have five loaves of bread and two fish." *(Show the five loaves and two fish to Jesus.)*

Jesus said, "Give them to me." *(Disciples give them to Jesus.)*

He took them *(take them),*

Looked up to heaven *(look up),*

Prayed over them *(hold up the loaves and fish),*

Put them in a basket *(put them in your basket),*

And said, "Give them to the people." *(Jesus says, "Give them to the people.")*

The disciples gave out the food. *(Disciples take Jesus' basket and give out the food to each person in the crowd.)*

The people ate until they were full. *(Pretend to eat the fish and loaves, then lean back and groan, "Oh, we're full.")*

Everyone was amazed because there were twelve baskets of food left over. *(Everyone says, "Wow!")*

After the story, have kids give themselves a standing ovation. Stand and clap and cheer!

Afterward SAY: **When we pray, God hears our prayers and answers them. We're going to learn more about prayer today.**

3. Fishy Snack

(You'll need fish-shaped crackers, juice, cups, and napkins.)

Tell children they're going to eat some food like the people did in the Bible story. Serve fish-shaped crackers, and distribute cups of juice. Pray before the snack, asking God to bless the food.

4. Prayer Topics

(You'll need photocopies of the "Prayer Topics" handout and crayons. Photocopy the handout on heavy paper.)

When kids finish their snack, give them each a "Prayer Topic" handout and some crayons. Explain the things we pray about that are shown on the handout: when we get hurt, when we're afraid, our family, someone who is sick, food.

SAY: **Color the pictures. Think about each thing as you color its picture. What else do you pray about? Draw those things in the blank squares. Maybe you have a problem with a friend or you're worried about your** parents. **God wants us to pray about all of our concerns.**

5. Prayer Bracelets

(You'll need safety scissors, a hole punch, and short pieces of yarn.)

Encourage children each to choose one thing they'd like to pray about today. Help each child cut that picture from the "Prayer Topics" handout.

Assist the children in punching a hole in each square and threading a short piece of yarn through the hole to make a bracelet. Loosely tie the prayer bracelet around the child's wrist. Make a bracelet for yourself, too.

6. Pray Always

Ask kids to gather in a circle. Help them memorize this paraphrase of 1 Thessalonians 5:16-18. You say a phrase and show an action. Then have children repeat what you say and do.

Be happy. *(Smile.)*

Pray always. *(Fold hands, bow heads.)*

Thank God for everything. *(Hold both hands up, look up to heaven.)*

After kids memorize the words and actions, do the actions and ask kids to supply the words.

Finally, have everyone do a silent version of the memorized verse. Have everyone do the actions only—no words.

7. God Listens

Have children sit on the floor in front of you. Show them your bracelet, and tell them what you want to pray about.

Tell children that they can pray to God and that he always listens. God wants us to tell him any problems or any concerns we have. He'll answer our prayers.

One at a time, ask children to show their bracelets and tell what they want to pray for.

After each child shares, all children say, "God listens when we pray" and pat their knees for each syllable.

8. Time to Pray

Take time to go around the circle and pray for the prayer concern of each child. If children are comfortable praying aloud, encourage them to do so. If a child is uncertain about praying aloud, let the child pray silently. After the children have prayed, close by praying: **Dear God, thank you for hearing our prayers. We trust you to answer them. Amen.**

9. Thank You, God

Remind kids that their memory verse said to pray always and thank God for everything.

One at a time, have kids say one thing they're thankful for. After each child says an item, have all kids clap and shout, "Thank you, God!" Let every person contribute, with the whole group shouting, "Thank you, God!" after each contribution.

by Christine Yount

What Is Prayer?

Actor 1: (Claps and jumps all around while looking up.)

Actor 2: (Enters) Hi. What are you doing?

Actor 1: (Keeps clapping.) Sh-h-h.

Actor 2: (Looks all around, confused. Then looks up.) Hey, what is it? Why are you clapping?

Actor 1: I'm not clapping.

Actor 2: Oh, yes, you are.

Actor 1: No, I'm not. I'm praying.

Actor 2: That's not praying. When you pray, you bow your head and you have to be quiet.

Actor 1: Yeah. I do that sometimes. But right now I'm just telling God how great I think he is. Why don't you join me? Yea, God!

Actor 2: (Joins and both say, "Yea, God!" and clap.)

Actor 2: Wait a minute. Wait a minute.

Actor 1: Now what?

Actor 2: I want to ask God a question. Is that OK?

Actor 1: Sure it is. That's part of prayer too.

Actor 2: You mean if we don't understand something, we can ask God about it in prayer?

Actor 1: Sure! God wants us to ask questions. So go ahead.

Actor 2: (Bows head, then looks up.) OK, I'm doing it.

Actor 1: Well, what'd you ask?

Actor 2: I asked God to teach me more about prayer because I like talking to him.

Fish and Loaves

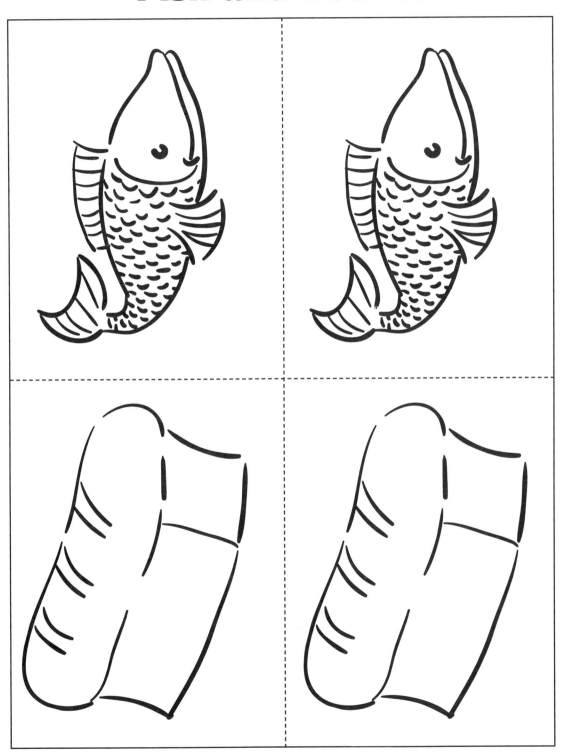

Prayer Topics

Prayer Topics

God's Gift—Forgiveness

A Powerful Purpose

Preschool children will learn that Jesus forgives us and wants us to forgive others.

A Look at the Lesson

A SPRINKLING OF SUPPLIES

- ❏ Bible
- ❏ masking tape
- ❏ paper
- ❏ marker
- ❏ colorful stickers
- ❏ paper plates
- ❏ napkins
- ❏ cups
- ❏ juice
- ❏ cheese and crackers
- ❏ photocopies of the handout (p. 76)
- ❏ crayons
- ❏ chairs
- ❏ CD of lively music
- ❏ CD player

We all feel guilty at times and are hard on ourselves. We wish we would've done things differently. We kick ourselves for saying something mean or selfish.

Preschoolers are not immune to guilt. They may feel sorry when they do something wrong, hurt their brothers or sisters, or hit their friends. Some innocent children feel guilty when their parents divorce.

Use this lesson to talk about the forgiveness Jesus offers.

THE LIVELY LESSON

1. Which Way Do I Go?

(Use masking tape to lay out two different "roads" on your floor as shown in the "Roads" diagram. Begin at your room's entrance and end up on the other side. Put a happy face on the wall at the end of one road and a sad face at the end of the other road.)

Greet each child and tell him or her to choose one of the roads and follow it to the end. SAY: **If you find a** happy face at the end of your road, sit down below the sign. If you find a sad face, go back and follow the other road.

When everyone is sitting under the happy face, give kids each a colorful sticker. SAY: **Sometimes we do bad things. That's like going down the wrong road. But if we do something bad, God will forgive us if we ask him to. Then we can continue on a good road by doing what's right. God's forgiveness makes us happy.**

2. A Bible Story

(You'll need a Bible.)

SAY: **Here's a Bible story about a son who took the wrong road and did the wrong thing. When the son felt bad for what he did, he told his father, "I'm sorry." His dad said, "It's OK. I love you." His dad forgave him.**

Read from a children's Bible the story of the prodigal son in Luke 15:11-24.

SAY: **God is like the father in the story who forgave his son. When the son admitted he had sinned, the father forgave him. God always forgives us when we ask for his forgiveness, and he wants us to forgive others who do bad things to us.**

Have children stand. Tell kids you're going to read some questions. If their answer is "happy," they should jump up and down and say "happy." If their answer is "sad," they should slowly sit down and say "sad."

Practice a couple times. Then read these questions:

• **At the end of the story, how do you think the dad felt when his boy returned home?**

• **At the beginning of the story, how do you think the dad felt about his son leaving?**

• **How do you think the younger son felt when he returned home and his dad welcomed him and forgave him?**

• **How do you feel when someone forgives you and says, "It's OK"?**

3. Banquet Time

(Prepare a table with paper plates, napkins, cups, juice, cheese, and crackers.)

ASK: **How do you feel knowing we're going to eat snacks and celebrate God's forgiveness?**

Since almost everyone should be jumping up and down and saying "happy," tell them they look like they would enjoy a forgiveness banquet—like the man gave his son in the story.

Lead them to the table and sit down for a meal. Distribute paper plates, napkins, and cups.

Pass around the cheese and crackers and SAY: **Eat some cheese and crackers. Fill up. God blesses us so much that we overflow with his goodness.**

Fill each cup with juice and SAY: **Drink this juice and remember that all good things—especially forgiveness—come from God.**

4. We Are All Forgiven

Play a post-banquet party game. Teach kids these words to the tune of "Ten Little Indians."

God forgives his little children,
God forgives his little children,
God forgives his little children,
When they say, "I'm sorry."

Gather in a circle and sing the song as you march clockwise. The second time you sing, have kids each find a partner, face each other, grab hands, and go sideways around the circle counterclockwise. The third time you sing, have everyone march clockwise again.

5. How Do You Feel?

(You'll need photocopies of the "How Do You Feel?" handout and crayons.)

Sit down in the circle after you finish the song. Give kids each a "How Do You Feel?" handout and crayons. Tell them to hold the handout so the face looks happy. Next, have them turn the handout upside down. The face now looks sad. Give children a couple of minutes to color the face.

SAY: **I'm going to ask you a few questions. If the answer is "happy," hold up the happy face. If it's "sad," turn the paper so the frowning face shows.**

ASK:

• **How do you feel after our banquet?**

• **How do you feel when someone hurts you?**

• **How do you feel when you forgive that person and say, "It's OK"?**

• **How would you feel if I said, "It's time to say goodbye"?**

• **How would you feel if I said, "We still have more fun activities to do, so we won't say goodbye for a while"?**

6. Forgive Others

(Each child will need the "How Do You Feel?" handout.)

SAY: **When God forgives us, we feel good. Others feel good when we forgive them. I'll read some stories, and you answer my questions by turning your paper to a smile or a frown, depending on your answer.**

• **Tiffany was playing with Tom's toy lawnmower and broke off one of its wheels. How does Tiffany feel? How does Tom feel?**

• **Tom got angry at Tiffany and made her go away. How does Tiffany feel? How does Tom feel?**

• **Tom said he would forgive Tiffany and gave Tiffany another toy to play with. How does Tiffany feel? How does Tom feel? How does God feel?**

• **Jeff, Chris, and Terry are playing together in the yard. How do they feel?**

• **Jeff and Chris ignore Terry and won't let her play with them. How does Terry feel?**

• **Terry gets mad and starts yelling. How does Terry feel?**

• **Jeff and Chris say they're sorry, and Terry forgives them. They keep playing. How does Terry feel? How does God feel? How do Jeff and Chris feel?**

7. Memory Tune

(You'll need a CD of lively music and a CD player.)

Let kids learn this Bible verse in a fun way: "Forgive each other" (Ephesians 4:32). Play lively music and ask kids to move around the room—hop, skip, walk, march, any movement they want. When you stop the music, have children each hug a person standing close to them and say, "Forgive each other." Start the music again and continue until kids have each hugged several different people and repeated the verse several times.

8. Musical Chairs

(You'll need chairs set up in a circle, enough for every child except one.)

Play a game of Musical Chairs, only don't eliminate anyone. Have children march around the chairs and sing the following song with you. When you stop singing, they should all sit down. One child will be without a seat. He or she should begin the song to start kids marching again. Sing the song to the tune of "London Bridge."

Say you're sorry when you're wrong,
when you're wrong,
when you're wrong.
Say you're sorry when you're wrong.
God forgives us.

by Ray and Cindy Peppers

How Do You Feel?

Heaven: Home, Sweet Home

A Powerful Purpose

Preschool children will learn that heaven is a place they'll like.

A Look at the Lesson

A SPRINKLING OF SUPPLIES

- ❏ Bible
- ❏ doll in a sack
- ❏ large pieces of construction paper
- ❏ crayons
- ❏ photocopies of the handout (p. 80)
- ❏ biscuits
- ❏ butter
- ❏ honey in squeeze bottles
- ❏ juice
- ❏ cups
- ❏ napkin
- ❏ supplies to clean hands

It is hard for a child to get a clear and reassuring picture of our eternal home. Simplify this concept by comparing heaven to the very best earthly home.

Use this lesson to show kids that though we don't know everything about heaven, we do know one important fact: Heaven will one day be our home, where we'll live with our heavenly Father and the wonderful family he has given us to love.

THE LIVELY LESSON

1. Squirrel at Home

Welcome the children and play a fun game to get them ready to learn. Choose one child to be an extra squirrel, then form teams of three with the rest of the kids. Have two members of each team make a "hollow tree" by standing facing each other, with their hands on each other's shoulders. Have the third team member play a "squirrel" by standing between the other two, at home in the tree. When you clap your hands, each squirrel must find a new home tree. The extra squirrel tries to find a home too. Whichever child is left out at the end of the run is the extra squirrel for the next time.

Play a few times, then switch roles so the "hollow trees" can be squirrels too. Rotate in any players who didn't get to play the first round.

SAY: **You all played squirrels at home in their trees. Our homes are in houses, apartments, or buildings. But today we're going to talk about heaven—our home when we go to live with Jesus forever.**

2. In a Sack

(You'll need a doll in a sack.)

Hold up the sack with the doll inside. Ask the children to describe the doll you're holding up. They may be able to guess that it has arms and legs and a face, but since they can't see it, they won't be able to describe it in detail.

Take the doll out of the bag. Hold it up so everyone can see it, then SAY: **Now tell me what the doll looks like.**

They'll tell you all they can see: hair color, eye color, what it's wearing. Pass around the doll while you discuss these questions:

• **Why couldn't you describe the doll when it was in a sack?**

• **Were there things you could guess about the doll even when you couldn't see it?**

SAY: **It's hard to describe something you can't see. That's just like heaven. It's hard to describe because we haven't seen it yet.**

3. Pictures of Home

(You'll need crayons and large pieces of construction paper. Lay them on the floor.)

Have kids follow you to the construction paper and crayons. As they follow you, march to the chant:

Heaven is a wonderful place;
It will be our home someday.

Have children each find a piece of paper to draw on. Tell them to draw pictures of their homes. When everyone has finished, take a walking tour around the pictures. As you walk and look, say the chant again.

4. What Makes a Home?

Let each child discuss his or her picture.

Adapt the following discussion depending on the children in your group. Be sensitive to kids whose homes might not be happy—through death or divorce or other reasons. Emphasize that heaven will be better than even the best earthly home.

SAY: **Our homes are special places. Most of us like our homes very much, and we wouldn't feel at home in any other house. Why is that? Is it because of the walls? the rooms? the windows? the furniture? All of our homes probably have these things. So there's nothing really special about them, is there? What does your home have that no other home has?**

Let kids try to guess, then SAY: **The people who live in our homes make our homes special.**

5. Heaven: Home, Sweet Home

(You'll need crayons and photocopies of the "Heaven: Home, Sweet Home" handout. Lay the handouts and crayons on the floor.)

Ask kids to follow behind you to another

area of the room where you've laid the handouts and crayons. As they follow, march to the same chant:

Heaven is a wonderful place;
It will be our home someday.

Read the handouts to the kids: "Heaven: Home, Sweet Home." Have them draw a picture of heaven as they imagine it—pretty clouds, warm sunshine, happy people.

After they finish, walk around their drawings as you say the chant again.

6. What Is Heaven?

(You'll need a Bible.)

SAY: **Heaven is God's home. Jesus lives there, and someday we will too. Listen as I read what Jesus says.**

Read John 14:3: **"And if I go and prepare a place for you, I will come back and take you to be with me that you also may be where I am."**

SAY: **You drew your ideas of heaven. Lots of people wonder what heaven will look like. But no one but God knows for sure. We haven't ever seen it. Remember how you couldn't describe the doll because you couldn't see it? Well, heaven is hard to describe too. But the Bible tells us about heaven.**

Read the following descriptions and direct kids to respond after each description.

• **Matthew 6:20 says we will have treasures in heaven.** (Have kids say, "O-o-o-o-o-o-o.")

• **John 14:2 says there are many rooms there for lots of people.** (Have kids spread their arms wide.)

• **Revelation 19:1 says that those who live in heaven will shout praises to God.** (Have everyone shout, "I love you, God!")

• **Revelation 21:3-4 says God will live with us there and will wipe all our tears away. There won't be any more crying or death or sadness.** (Have everyone smile big smiles.)

So heaven will one day be the home where God lives with all of us, his children. (Have everyone link arms in a circle and sit down.)

7. Heavenly Honey Biscuits

(You'll need biscuits, butter, honey in squeeze bottles, juice, cups, napkins, and supplies to clean hands.)

Serve biscuits, butter, honey, and juice. Then PRAY: **Thank you, God, that you're making a wonderful home for us in heaven. Thank you for loving us so much that you want to live there with us forever. Amen.**

Sing songs such as "Heaven Is a Wonderful Place" and "Do, Lord."

Let kids take home their two drawings—their earthly home and their heavenly home.

by Karen M. Ball

Heaven:
Home, Sweet Home

Part 4: A Lively Look at celebrations

A Birthday Bonanza

A Powerful Purpose

Preschool children will celebrate their birthdays and see that the bigger they grow, the more they know.

A Look at the Lesson

A SPRINKLING OF SUPPLIES

- ❏ Bible
- ❏ baby-size doll
- ❏ bright color of tempera paint
- ❏ flat pans
- ❏ old shirts or smocks
- ❏ colored construction paper
- ❏ photocopies of the handout (p. 85)
- ❏ balloons
- ❏ frosted cupcakes

For each child, you'll need one item of baby or adult clothing.

Preschool children are learning about themselves, especially about what they can do. They're in a concrete stage of learning and don't understand symbolism. Each new learning experience (especially when presented in an active, fun way) provides important information about their capabilities and enhances self-esteem.

Use this lesson to show kids how much they're growing and how they're learning new things.

THE LIVELY LESSON

1. Babies Can't Do This

As children arrive, seat them in a circle. Ask them, one by one: **What can you do that a baby can't do? Show me!** For example, they can run, jump, talk, hop, or sing.

After each child shows you something, SAY: **When you were a baby, you couldn't do these things. Now you can because you're growing.**

2. My Handprints: I Am Growing

(You'll need the baby-size doll, bright color of tempera paint in flat pans, photocopies of the "My Handprints" handout, old shirts or smocks. Ask someone to help you with this activity.)

Pass around the doll, and ask the children each to hold their hands up to the doll's hand. SAY: **Something else that tells us we're growing is that we get bigger. Look at your hands and see how much bigger they are than the doll's hands. Are your hands bigger than a baby's hands?**

Tell them they're going to make prints of their hands, which are bigger than a baby's but still smaller than a grown-up's.

Hold up a "My Handprints" handout and read the poem.

> **Here are handprints of me,**
> **Made for people to see.**
> **Though to you I seem small,**
> **God will help me grow tall!**

Cover the kids' good clothes with the old shirts or smocks. Help children dip the palms of their hands in the tempera paint and press them firmly on their handouts. Have someone help the children wash their hands afterward. Write each child's name on his or her paper.

3. Birthday Balloons: Getting Bigger and Bigger

(You'll need an inflated balloon for each person.)

SAY: **We use balloons to celebrate birthdays. But did you know that a balloon can grow like your body grows?**

Show kids a deflated balloon, then SAY: **See how small this balloon is? Watch what**

happens to it.

Blow into the balloon until it's one-fourth full. SAY: **This balloon is like a one-year-old.** Add a bit more air and SAY: **Now it's like a two-year-old.** And so on, until the balloon is "like a five-year-old." SAY: **This balloon grew just as you are growing. I'm going to give you each a balloon. We're going to bat the balloons in the air.**

Give one inflated balloon to each child and allow a couple minutes of "balloon-batting." The goal is that the balloons stay in the air. As kids bat balloons, lead them in saying, "Growing, growing, we are growing."

After balloons have been batted for a while, gather them. If any balloon breaks, immediately pick up all pieces.

4. Happy Birthday to Me

Gather kids in a circle around you. SAY: **One thing that happens when we grow is that we have birthdays!** Ask children to stand in groups by indicating that three-year-olds should stand in front of you, four-year-olds to one side, and so on.

Then lead everyone in shouting at the same time: **Happy birthday to me!** Shout several times, increasing the volume, then have children wish each other "happy birthday" and sit down.

5. Birthday Party Snack

(You'll need frosted cupcakes, one for each child.)

Pass out the frosted cupcakes as you SAY: **Happy birthday, birthday kids. Have some birthday cake.**

6. Jesus Grew Too

(You'll need a Bible.)

While kids are eating, SAY: **Did you know**

that Jesus was once a child too? We celebrate his birthday at Christmas. After Jesus was a baby, he grew to be your age. Listen to what the Bible tells us.

Read Luke 2:52 from a children's Bible, or use this wording: **"Jesus continued to learn more and more and to grow physically. People liked him, and he pleased God."**

SAY: **Jesus grew up as a child just like you're growing up.**

After kids swallow the last of their cupcakes, SAY: **Let's sing Jesus a birthday song too.** Sing these words:

Happy birthday to you,
Happy birthday to you,
Happy birthday, dear Jesus,
We sure do love you!

7. I'm Not a Baby, I'm Not a Grown-Up

(Place the baby and adult clothes in the center of the room.)

Gather children in a circle around the clothes. One at a time, have each child pick out one item of clothing and take it back to his or her seat.

After everyone has done this, go around the circle and invite kids to try on their chosen items. Ask children questions such as: **What's wrong with that item? How does it feel? Is it too big or too small?**

With each item of baby clothing, say something like: **Those baby clothes are too small for you.** With each item of adult clothing say something like: **Those grown-up clothes are too big for you.**

After everyone has had a turn, SAY: **As you can see, you're no longer babies, but** you're not yet grown-ups. You are you. Right now. Each of you is a special person. You're growing bigger each day, and you'll keep growing. Each inch you grow, each day of your life, you learn new things. That's the way God made you.

8. See How Tall I Grow to Be

Sing this action song to the tune of "Twinkle, Twinkle, Little Star." Have children repeat each line with actions, then slowly combine all lines together.

See how tall I grow to be. *(Stretch hands above head.)*

Inch by inch I grow, you see. *(Stretch hands above head "inch by inch" with each word.)*

I'm not a baby anymore. *(Rock baby.)*

I'm getting bigger, that's for sure. *(Jump.)*

See how tall I grow to be. *(Stretch on toes.)*

God made you *(point to others)*,

And God made me. *(Point to self.)*

9. Thanks for Birthdays and Growing

Ask children to hold hands in a circle and bow their heads. PRAY: **Thank you, God, for making me and for giving me a family that loves me. Thank you for each birthday and that I am growing each day. Amen.**

Give kids their balloons to take home. As you hand out the balloons SAY: **Happy Birthday!**

by Jerayne Gray-Reneberg

My Handprints

Here are handprints of me,
Made for people to see.
Though to you I seem small,
God will help me grow tall!

The Reason for Easter

A Powerful Purpose

Preschool children will learn more
about Jesus and about Easter.

A Look at the Lesson

1. Class Crier . . . . . . (Interspersed throughout the meeting)
2. Jesus Died for My Sins . . . . (up to 4 minutes)
3. Resurrection Buns . . . . (up to 6 minutes)
4. The Easter Story . . . . (up to 5 minutes)
5. Eyewitness Report . . . . (up to 6 minutes)
6. Up, Up, Up. . . . . (up to 4 minutes)
7. Easter Baskets. . . . . (up to 7 minutes)
8. Easter Cross Hunt . . . . (up to 6 minutes)
9. Prayer Time . . . . (up to 2 minutes)

A SPRINKLING OF SUPPLIES:

- Bible or a book for children that tells the Easter story
- two Resurrection Buns per child
- sandwich bags
- photocopies of the handouts (pp. 89-90)
- three puppets made from socks or bags
- cardboard
- marker
- tape
- stapler and staples
- table
- Easter stickers
- construction paper
- scissors
- one plastic gallon milk jug per child

E aster can mean a lot of things to young children: Easter egg hunts, baskets, and bunnies. Easter can also mean a time of big meals, family gatherings, church services, and songs.

Use this lesson to help children talk about Easter. Help them focus on the real reason for Easter—Jesus.

THE LIVELY LESSON

1. Class Crier

(Ask an adult or teenager to perform as the class crier four times during the lesson. Read the lesson ahead of time to see when the class crier walks through. The person should dress like a follower of Jesus.)

When children have arrived, have the class crier give the first cry: "Oh, my. Jesus is dead. He died on a cross."

Welcome the kids and SAY: **That was our class crier**

who'll tell us Easter messages throughout our time together.

2. Jesus Died for My Sins

Ask kids to join hands in a circle and walk clockwise as they sing this song to the tune of "London Bridge."

**Jesus died for my sins,
For my sins,
For my sins;
Jesus died for my sins,
I'm forgiven.**

Have kids sing the song several times, then sit down in a circle. SAY: **We're going to talk about Easter—about Jesus dying for our sins, or the wrong things we do, and rising from the dead. When Jesus died on a cross, he was buried in a tomb, which is a cave for people who have died.**

Have the class crier cry a second time: "Oh, no. Jesus is buried in a tomb."

SAY: **But that's not the end of the story.**

3. Resurrection Buns

(You'll need Resurrection Buns made according to the recipe on the handout.)

Give each child a Resurrection Bun. As kids bite into their buns, they'll discover that the buns' hollow insides contain a sugary surprise.

SAY: **You're surprised at the inside of your Resurrection Bun. The disciples were also surprised on the first Easter. They went inside the tomb where Jesus was buried and discovered something. It was empty.**

Have the class crier give the third cry: "I'm so sad that Jesus is dead."

4. The Easter Story

(You'll need a children's Bible or a book that tells the Easter story for children.)

Read the Easter story from John 20:1-8 or from a children's book.

Ask kids to close their eyes and picture the story in their minds. Imagine…
• early morning
• going to the tomb
• seeing that the big rock used to cover the opening was rolled away
• Mary running to tell the others
• Peter and the other disciple running back to the tomb
• seeing the tomb was empty
• Jesus was not there

Have the class crier enter the room quietly and cry out the fourth time: "He's alive! He's alive! He's alive!"

5. Eyewitness Report

(You'll need the "Eyewitness Report" skit and three puppets—a reporter and two disciples. Make simple puppets out of socks or paper bags. Use a marker to design faces. Tape a cardboard microphone to the front of the reporter puppet. Ask three helpers to perform this puppet skit. Turn a table on its side and use it for a stage.)

Have everyone follow the class crier around the room. Everyone marches behind the crier, chanting, "He's alive! He's alive! He's alive!" The class crier leads them over to the puppet stage.

When kids are seated, begin the "Eyewitness Report" puppet show.

6. Up, Up, Up

After the puppet show, SAY: **We're going**

to celebrate that surprising report that Jesus is alive. He rose from the dead.

Teach children this Easter action song to the tune of "Row, Row, Row Your Boat." Repeat the song and actions several times.

Up (touch the floor),
Up (touch your thighs),
Up (touch your shoulders)
He rose (wave hands above head);
Jesus is alive. (Clap, clap, clap.)
Jesus is alive today. (Wave hands above head.)
Jesus is alive. (Clap, clap, clap.)

7. Easter Baskets

(For each child, you'll need an empty plastic gallon milk jug. You'll also need scissors, a stapler and Easter stickers. Cut the gallon jugs in half. Before class, cut a 1-inch ring from the bottom of the upper half of the jug. Clip the ring to make a strip of plastic.)

Give each child a strip of plastic and a lower half of a milk jug. Show children how to staple the strip on as a handle, and help them do this. Then let children use the stickers to decorate their baskets.

Note: You can also follow this example

and use a medium-sized paper bag to make a paper basket for each child.

8. Easter Cross Hunt

(For each child, you'll need three construction paper crosses.)

While kids finish decorating their baskets, hide the crosses in the room.

SAY: **Since Jesus is the real reason for Easter, we're not going to look for Easter eggs today; we're going to look for Easter crosses. We're celebrating because Jesus died on a cross and lives again.**

Let kids hunt for the Easter crosses and put them in their baskets. Then let kids take turns hiding the crosses and letting others hunt for them. After your game, divide the crosses evenly among the children.

9. Prayer Time

(For each child, you'll need a photocopy of the "Resurrection Buns" handout and a Resurrection Bun in a sandwich bag.)

After the hunt, gather the children. Instead of forming a circle, form a cross. PRAY: **Thank you, Jesus, for dying for us on a cross and for rising from the dead on Easter. Amen.**

Give kids each a photocopy of the "Resurrection Bun" handout, and put a wrapped Resurrection Bun in each child's basket. Let kids take their baskets home and have a wonderful Easter.

by Christine Yount

Resurrection Buns

Frozen bread dough
Butter
24 marshmallows
1 cup sugar
2 teaspoons cinnamon

Let the frozen dough thaw.

Melt some butter.

In a separate bowl, mix the sugar and cinnamon together.

Divide dough into 24 uniform balls. Roll each ball out until flat. Wrap each flattened ball around a marshmallow, making sure to seal all openings. Dip the ball in melted butter, then in the sugar and cinnamon mixture.

Place in a large, greased baking pan. Cover and let rise until double (about 35 minutes). Bake at 375° for 18 to 20 minutes. Makes 24.

Eyewitness Report

The reporter puppet stands on the stage. Two disciple puppets run across the stage and almost knock the reporter over.

Reporter: Hey, what's going on here?

Disciple 1: Haven't you heard the news?

Disciple 2: I thought everyone knew by now!

Reporter: What news? Knew what? *(Points microphone toward each puppet's face as he talks.)*

Disciple 1: He's alive!

Disciple 2: He has risen!

Reporter: What? Are you saying a dead person is now alive?

Both: Yes! Jesus is alive! *(Reporter is confused about where to point the microphone.)*

Reporter: Jesus? Who is this "Jesus"?

Disciple 1: He is the Son of God.

Reporter: And you say he died. How did this "Jesus" die?

Disciple 2: It was three days ago. The saddest day of our lives.

Disciple 1: They hung Jesus on a cross and killed him.

Reporter: What did he do wrong?

Disciple 1: Nothing. They just wanted to kill him.

Disciple 2: And he died. And we thought it was all over.

Disciple 1: But today we saw him! We saw his hands and feet where the nails had been.

Reporter: A dead man is alive? How?

Disciple 1: God raised him from the dead.

Reporter: Why did God raise Jesus from the dead?

Disciple 2: So we can live forever, just like Jesus!

Reporter: What?

Disciple 1: Don't you see? Jesus is God's gift to us. If we accept God's gift of Jesus, we'll live forever too.

Reporter: *(Turns to audience.)* Well, you heard it, folks. Jesus was killed and buried in a tomb for three days. But now he's alive. This is Perry Puppet reporting live from Jerusalem on Easter morning.

A Thankful Thanksgiving

A Powerful Purpose

Preschool children will give thanks,
as the pilgrims did, for blessings in their lives.

A Look at the Lesson

1. God Loves Me Every Day . . . . (up to 5 minutes)
2. Shake a Story . . . . (up to 6 minutes)
3. Pat a Pilgrim's Prayer . . . . (up to 3 minutes)
4. Friendship Feast . . . . (up to 6 minutes)
5. Seeds Are Beautiful . . . . (up to 6 minutes)
6. We Give Thanks . . . . (up to 6 minutes)
7. Great Growth Charts . . . . (up to 6 minutes)
8. God's Love Keeps Growing . . . . (up to 2 minutes)

A SPRINKLING OF SUPPLIES

- ❏ Bible
- ❏ one pint of cold heavy whipping cream
- ❏ one see-through plastic container with a tight-fitting lid
- ❏ crackers
- ❏ knife
- ❏ small bowl
- ❏ chocolate milk
- ❏ different types of seeds (pumpkin, sunflower, sesame, apple)
- ❏ different colors of construction paper
- ❏ glue
- ❏ tape measure
- ❏ butcher paper
- ❏ marker
- ❏ crayons
- ❏ straight pins
- ❏ bulletin board

Young children are interested in doing things with their friends. They also love to hear stories—especially stories that happened long ago or "Once upon a time..."

Use this lesson to help preschoolers learn about Thanksgiving. Give them an opportunity to thank God for blessings in their lives.

THE LIVELY LESSON

1. God Loves Me Every Day

Greet the children, then gather in a circle. Tell them they're going to learn about Thanksgiving and have a chance to give thanks for their blessings.

Teach children this song to the tune of "Twinkle, Twinkle, Little Star." Have them repeat, line by line with actions, then slowly combine all lines together.

I know God loves me every day. *(Hug self.)*

God shows me in many ways *(arms extended, separated lightly, palms up)*:

My family and the friends I meet *(hands over heart)*

And the good food that I eat. *(Touch lips.)*

God's good blessings with me stay. *(Arms raised, palms open.)*

I know God loves me every day. *(Hug self.)*

2. Shake a Story

(Pour the cold heavy whipping cream into the see-through container with a tight-fitting lid. Shake the container for five to six minutes to begin the butter-making process. Kids will continue to shake during the activity—approximately two to three more minutes.)

Pass around the container filled with heavy whipping cream. Explain that the kids will take turns shaking the container to make butter while you tell the story of the pilgrims.

Once upon a time, long ago, the pilgrims came to America. These people came from across the sea. When they got here, though, they didn't know how to grow foods in a new land. So the Indians showed them how to grow things like corn, pumpkins, and beans and how to prepare and eat turkey. Without the Indians' help, the pilgrims would have had little to eat and would have starved.

The first year, when all the foods were ready to eat, the pilgrims had a big feast and invited their Indian friends. They thanked God for all the delicious new foods and for their new friends. And each Thanksgiving Day, we do the same thing

when we thank God for food, friends, families, and all the gifts God gives us.

SAY: **Today we'll celebrate our own Friendship Feast with the butter you've just been making. Let's thank God for our butter and all our blessings.**

Set the forming butter aside.

3. Pat a Pilgrim's Prayer

Ask kids to pat their knees in rhythm. Tell them they're going to pat a prayer to a one-two beat. Ask the kids to repeat each line after you say it. Keep the patting rhythm going throughout the prayer.

Thank you, God,
For these gifts:
Food,
Families,
Friends,
Our beautiful earth,
Us,
Jesus.
He sure loves us.
He calls us friends.
Amen!

4. Friendship Feast

(You'll need a Bible, the butter, crackers, a bowl, and a butter knife.)

Help the children remove the lid from the container. Pour off the liquid into the empty bowl. Spread on crackers. Also serve chocolate milk or another drink kids will be thankful for.

SAY: **There's a Bible verse that's nice for Thanksgiving. Listen to it as you eat your crackers and butter.**

Read Psalm 107:1 from a children's Bible, or use this wording: **"Thank the Lord because he is good. His love continues forever!"**

5. Seeds Are Beautiful

(You'll need construction paper, glue, and seeds.)

Tell kids they're going to make seed pictures by gluing seeds onto construction paper. Older kids may want to glue seeds in the shape of the earth, their friends, their families, their pets, their churches, their homes, or whatever they're thankful for. Others may want to create a free design. Let the children glue seeds on their paper in any way they choose.

SAY: **Seeds are one thing to thank God for. We can use them for food or plant them to grow more food.**

6. We Give Thanks

(You'll need straight pins and a bulletin board titled "We Give Thanks.")

Gather in a circle. Ask the children to show their pictures and explain what they're thankful for. After the glue dries, pin the pictures to the bulletin board titled "We Give Thanks." Read the bulletin board title to the kids.

7. Great Growth Charts

(Make growth charts by cutting 6-inch-by-2-feet butcher paper strips, one for each child. With a marker, mark 1-inch measurements along the side. Start at the bottom with 24 inches and go up to 48 inches. You'll also need crayons.)

SAY: **Food is not the only thing that grows. What else grows that we're thankful for?**

SAY: **There are lots of things that grow. Even you! Now we're going to make growth charts so you can measure how much you grow.**

Give each child a growth chart prepared earlier. Let kids decorate their charts to take home and hang on their walls.

Help them measure their present height. Tell kids to thank God for his measureless, endless love each time they measure their growth.

8. God's Love Keeps Growing

(You'll need the completed growth charts.)

Ask children to bring their competed growth charts and gather in a circle. For a closing prayer, begin with: **Thanks, God, for your love that keeps growing...** Have kids, one at a time, say "and growing" as they hold up their growth chart. Continue around the circle so each child has a chance to add to the prayer. When it gets back to you, SAY: **Amen!**

by Jerayne Gray-Reneberg

Christmas Celebration

A Powerful Purpose

Preschool children will relate their own experiences with babies to the baby Jesus of long ago.

A Look at the Lesson

1. Baby Hide-and-Seek . . . . (up to 5 minutes)
2. What Do You Know About Babies? . . . (up to 3 minutes)
3. Action-Packed Story . . . . (up to 4 minutes)
4. Snackin' Time . . . . (up to 3 minutes)
5. Jesus' Birthday . . . . (up to 3 minutes)
6. Wrapping Baby Jesus . . . . (up to 6 minutes)
7. Rattle Rhymes. . . . . (up to 4 minutes)
8. Christmas Singalong . . . . (up to 5 minutes)
9. Christmas Prayer . . . . (up to 2 minutes)

Babies, babies everywhere. All of us were once babies. The Christmas story tells of Jesus' birth and the miraculous events surrounding the beginning of this special baby's life.

Use this lesson to show similarities and differences between babies now and the baby Jesus on the first Christmas.

THE LIVELY LESSON

1. Baby Hide-and-Seek

(On a table place a diaper, baby rattle, baby powder, ointment, booties, and one receiving blanket.)

Welcome the children and gather around the table. SAY: **Today we're going to talk about babies. And we're going to learn about a special baby—Jesus.**

Discuss the items on the table and how they're used for babies. Then cover the items with the receiving

A SPRINKLING OF SUPPLIES

- ❐ diaper
- ❐ baby rattle
- ❐ baby powder
- ❐ ointment
- ❐ booties
- ❐ receiving blanket
- ❐ spoons
- ❐ napkins
- ❐ Bible
- ❐ photocopies of the handout (p. 97)
- ❐ scrap fabric cut in strips
- ❐ crayons
- ❐ glue sticks
- ❐ pots
- ❐ pans
- ❐ lids
- ❐ bowls
- ❐ baby-food jars (optional)

For each child, you'll also need applesauce and a baby rattle.

blanket. Ask children to cover their eyes while you remove one item. Uncover the items and see if children can name the missing one. Play this game several times, but quit before children lose interest.

2. What Do You Know About Babies?

Gather in a circle, sit down, and discuss:
• How many of you have a baby in your home?
• How many of you have played with a baby?
• What do babies do?
• Where are babies born?
• What can you tell me about Jesus when he was a baby?
• What do we call the special day when Jesus was born?

SAY: **Babies do all kinds of things. They giggle.** (Ask kids to giggle.) **They cry.** (Ask kids to pretend to cry.) **They like to be hugged.** (Tell kids each to hug the people sitting on both sides of them.)

Jesus was a baby too. He giggled, cried, and liked to be hugged. He was born long ago in a town called Bethlehem. We celebrate his birthday on Christmas.

3. Action-Packed Story

Ask children to stand. Lead them in the following action-packed Christmas story.

Jesus and Mary had to take a trip on a donkey. (Walk in place, pretend to pull a stubborn donkey.)

Joseph and Mary looked for a place to stay. (Look around, up high, down low, under things.)

The innkeeper had no room for them. (Shake head.)

Mary and Joseph slept on the stable floor. (Lie on the floor.)

When Jesus was born, they wrapped him up. (Pretend to wrap a baby and cuddle him.)

Mary laid him in a manger. (Pretend to lay baby down.)

Mary and Joseph thanked God. (Fold hands, look to heaven.)

4. Snackin' Time

(You'll need applesauce—served in baby-food jars if possible—spoons, and napkins.)

Ask kids to follow you to a snack table. March to this chant:

**Time, time, time to eat.
Follow me to a little treat!**

Have children think about babies who eat real baby food from the jars.

5. Jesus' Birthday

(You'll need a children's Bible.)

Tell children to continue eating their snack and listen to a story about the very first Christmas. Read Luke 2:1-20. ASK:
• What town was Jesus born in?
• Where did he sleep?
• What did he wear?

SAY: **Jesus was born in a place where they kept animals—something like a barn. His bed was a manger—what they used to hold food for animals. He wore cloths that wrapped all around him to keep him warm.**

6. Wrapping Baby Jesus

(You'll need the "Baby Jesus" handout, scrap fabric cut in strips, crayons, and glue sticks.)

Ask kids to follow you to the

table with the supplies. Tell them they're going to remember that first Christmas—baby Jesus' birthday—by wrapping Jesus in swaddling clothes.

Give each child a "Baby Jesus" handout. Have kids color baby Jesus' face. Then help them glue the fabric strips to Jesus' body.

7. Rattle Rhymes

(You'll need one baby rattle for each child.)

Give each child a baby rattle. Read the following word groups. In each group, have the children listen for the word that relates to Jesus' birth. When they hear one, kids should shake their rattle. Do the first one or two with them.

Ball, <u>baby</u>, bubble
Bowl, bicycle, <u>Bethlehem</u>
Caterpillar, <u>Christmas</u>, cartwheel
Minnie, Mollie, <u>Mary</u>
Monkey, <u>manger</u>, Montana
<u>God</u>, golf, green

SAY: **Jesus was a real baby, a lot like babies you've seen. And he is also God. He came to earth as a baby and then grew up to save us from our sins.**

8. Christmas Singalong

(You'll need pots, pans, lids, spoons, and bowls—anything that can be used as a musical instrument.)

Show children the variety of kitchen utensils. Invite them each to create a musical instrument, make a sound, or beat a rhythm and then practice. For example, hit two lids together, click two spoons together, use a spoon to tap on a bowl or pan.

Sing some of the kids' favorite Christmas songs such as "Away in a Manger" and "Joy to the World." Direct the instrumentalists to play as they sing.

9. Christmas Prayer

Ask kids to hold their instruments quietly as you pray. You'll signal them to "make a joyful noise" at the end of the prayer.

PRAY: **Thanks for babies, God. Thanks especially for baby Jesus and his birthday—Christmas.**

Ask kids to play their instruments as they shout, "Merry Christmas!"

by Nanette Goings

Baby Jesus

Children's Ministry Leadership

Children's Ministry Leadership: The You-Can-Do-It Guide

Jim Wideman

You can be a next-level leader! Expert Jim Wideman empowers readers to be dynamic, effective and efficient ministry leaders. This guide gives you the best of the best from Jim's favorite workshops and keynote addresses he's presented. And this isn't just theory—it's practical advice brought to you from someone who has served in hundreds of children's ministry settings, both behind the scenes and on stage.

ISBN 0-7644-2527-7

Jim Wideman is a warm and engaging speaker on effective children's ministry. He is a children's pastor and director of Christian education at Church On the Move in Tulsa, Oklahoma. Wideman leads Kids On the Move, which hosts more than 75 classes for kids per week and is fueled by a team of more than 900 volunteers.

Children's Ministry That Works! (Revised and Updated)

For over 10 years, *Children's Ministry That Works* has been helping ministry leaders create dynamic and effective ministry programs in churches across the country. Now, completely revised and updated, this new version will help you be successful for the next 10 years! You'll get the best, proven-effective ideas and strategies from 27 top children's leaders, including Craig Jutila, Jim Wideman, Christine Yount, Pat Verbal, and others. 15 brand-new chapters offer help for key areas of children's ministry, including developing your leadership team, partnering with parents, teaching so children can learn, and more! Great for new or veteran children's ministers!

ISBN 0-7644-2407-6

Leadership Essentials for Children's Ministry

Craig Jutila

Craig Jutila and his team have built one of the most significant, cutting-edge children's ministries in the world at Saddleback Church. In this book, he shares with you leadership insights that will build powerful leadership skills in you and your team based on four critical foundational principles:

Passion—It is essential to approach ministry as an energizing act of worship, not a chore.

Attitude—Our mindset determines our level of happiness and satisfaction within our ministry.

Teamwork—To succeed in leadership we must link up with those whose gifts can support and complement our own.

Honor—To grow and keep ministry enjoyable we must serve in an atmosphere of mutual respect and encouragement.

In *Leadership Essentials for Children's Ministry*, learn from one of America's top children's ministry leaders how to build (or rebuild) a purpose-driven children's ministry in your church.

ISBN 0-7644-2389-4

Craig Jutila is the Children's Pastor at Saddleback Church in Lake Forest, California. Craig is an author and sought-after motivational communicator with intensely practical insights. He is also the Founder of Empoweringkids.net, a company designed to provide relevant resources for children's leaders in the local church.

For the Teacher

Teacher Training on the Go

Keith Johnson

Train—and retain—volunteers. This is instant teacher training volunteers desperately need! A year's worth of reproducible training handouts helps volunteers be their best. Their skills and effectiveness in children's ministry will grow. Includes:

- 1 audio CD
- 52 reproducible handouts
- 1 CD-ROM with e-mail blasts & clip art
- "Meeting format," appendix, and topic index
- BONUS: Reproducible audio CD empowers volunteers as they drive to church!

ISBN 0-7644-2548-X

Keith Johnson is the National Field Services Manager for Group Publishing in Loveland, CO. Keith oversees a team of nearly 150 REAL Learning Specialists who conduct more than 1,000 teacher training events yearly. He is a graduate of Dallas Theological Seminary and has been a children's pastor for 16 years, most recently at Wooddale Church in Eden Prairie, MN. Keith was also the Director of Children's Ministries for the International Division of the Billy Graham Evangelistic Association.

Heartfelt Thanks™ for Sunday School Teachers

How do you truly thank Sunday school teachers in a way that shows deep appreciation, encouragement and inspiration? Give them *Heartfelt Thanks!* Packed with vibrant full-color art, *Heartfelt Thanks for Sunday School Teachers* includes space for journaling and responding to ministry questions. This portable keepsake is a memorable and inspirational gift—have extras on hand to give away when someone needs encouragement. Here's why this perfect gift builds team members:

- **Inspiration**—Sunday school teachers share real-life stories
- **Scripture**—Verses encourage
- **Reflection**—Journal space for devotional thoughts & responses

Great for individual worship and devotional activities!

ISBN 0-7644-2433-5

Heartfelt Thanks™ for Helping Kids Love Jesus

Looking for a special way to express genuine appreciation to Sunday school teachers? Give them *Heartfelt Thanks!* This vibrant devotional is packed with heartwarming stories by seasoned teachers that reinforce the remarkable difference that can be made in the lives of students—even when no one seems to notice! Each inspirational account concludes with a personal prayer or devotional activity that injects a fresh perspective and rekindles a passion for fostering spiritual growth in children. It's the perfect gift!

ISBN 0-7644-2638-9

The Encyclopedia of Bible Crafts for Children

Includes nearly 200 easy craft ideas that connect children with Bible truths in a memorable way. Crafts for every major Bible story and book of the Bible! Scripture and topic indexes make it easy to find just the right craft. Indexes for Faith-Weaver™, Hands-On Bible Curriculum™, and FaithWeaver Friends™ coordinate crafts with those Bible curricula!

Reproducibles included!
ISBN 0-7644-2395-9

The Children's Worker's Encyclopedia of Bible-Teaching Ideas

Over 340 attention-grabbing, active-learning devotions...art and craft projects...creative prayers...service projects...field trips...music suggestions...quiet reflection activities...skits... and more—winning ideas from each book of the Bible.

Old Testament	**ISBN 1-55945-622-1**
New Testament	**ISBN 1-55945-625-6**

Children's Ministry Must-Haves

Playful Songs & Bible Stories for Preschoolers

You'll find one sweet song, one funtastic finger play and one interactive story reading for each of the 75 most important Bible stories. Songs such as "Silly Adam" delight preschoolers as they learn Bible points. And everyone has fun with the hand motions! Help little ones learn lyrics…teachers will find the two CDs helpful because one includes words and music and the other includes just the words. Scripture and topic indexes make lesson planning easy! Sheet music not included.

ISBN 0-7644-2534-X

Pray & Play Bible for Young Children

This Bible story and activity book is certain to become a classic! 14 favorite Bible stories are beautifully bound in a large 9 x 12 hardcover book complete with 4-color artwork throughout. The child-friendly language makes it perfect for your church nursery and preschool classes. This is a memory-making activity book—with 3 pages of activities, snack ideas, games, crafts, and songs after each story. Children will experience and remember each important Bible story.

ISBN 0-7644-2024-0

Pray & Play Bible 2

It's finally here! Many have asked for a follow-up to the best-selling nursery classic, *Pray & Play Bible for Young Children*. So, we're excited to release an additional 14 favorite Bible stories. This large 9" x 12" hardcover, beautifully adorned with full-color artwork throughout, creates lively story time. Each Bible story includes 10 activities to make memorable messages—crafts, games, story enhancements, affirmations, service projects, singing, ideas, and more. Whether it's used at church or home, children will experience Bible stories in unforgettable ways:
• Easy, child-friendly language makes *Pray & Play* a joy to use
• Large format is an instant eye-pleaser
• Includes 140 activities to connect with the stories!

ISBN 0-7644-2514-5

Instant Puppet Skits: 20 Stories From People Who Met Jesus

John Cutshall & Mikal Keefer

These 20 quick-prep puppet skits are sure to engage children and adults. Each puppet show is enhanced with the dialogue and sound effects found on two long-play CDs. Children interact with puppets as the characters highlight important Bible stories about Jesus, told by witty, fun-loving puppets who've just "met" Jesus. Includes stage directions, backgrounds and photocopiable props. Teach kids about Jesus in a captivating, clever and memorable way!

ISBN 0-7644-2458-0

John Cutshall is a seasoned minister, speaker, radio personality and writer. Formerly a Bible college dean, he continues to minister to families through the local church.

Mikal Keefer has developed puppet scripts for several publishers, dozens of churches and boatloads of children. He is Group Publishing's senior editor of children's books.

Puppet Ministry Made Easy

Dale and Liz VonSeggen

Have you always wanted to try puppet ministry? Or maybe you want fresh ideas for your existing team? This comprehensive guide is a great place to start!

Learn how to:
• Recruit the right people• Plan tours
• Organize your ministry• Make stages
• Write your own • Rehearse
  puppet scripts• And more!

Includes 9 ready-to-use scripts written by leading experts in puppet ministry. Create a powerful team-building outreach for both children and adults!

ISBN 0-7644-2525-0

Dale VonSeggen is co-founder and president of One Way Street, Inc., a children's ministry resource publisher. He served as a children's pastor for nine years and, together with Liz, has co-directed a puppet team for 22 years.

Liz VonSeggen is co-founder and director of new product development for One Way Street. An accomplished ventriloquist, she and Dale have published hundreds of puppet plays, puppet songs and puppet ministry training resources used worldwide.

EVALUATION FOR
Lively Bible Lessons for Preschoolers

Please help Group Publishing, Inc., continue to provide innovative and useful resources for ministry. Please take a moment to fill out this evaluation and mail or fax it to us. Thanks!

Group Publishing, Inc.
Attention: Product Development
P.O. Box 481
Loveland, CO 80539
Fax: (970) 292-4370

1. As a whole, this book has been (circle one)
   not very helpful   *very helpful*
   1   2   3   4   5   6   7   8   9   10

2. The best things about this book:

3. Ways this book could be improved:

4. Things I will change because of this book:

5. Other books I'd like to see Group publish in the future:

6. Would you be interested in field-testing future Group products and giving us your feedback? If so, please fill in the information below:

Name _____

Church Name _____

Denomination _____ Church Size _____

Church Address _____

City _____ State _____ ZIP _____

Church Phone _____

E-mail _____